GOD

WANTS YOU RICH

NOT POOR & STRUGGLING

SCOT ANDERSON

DESTINY IMAGE® PUBLISHERS, INC.

P.O. Box 310, Shippensburg, PA 17257-0310

"Speaking to the Purposes of God for This Generation and for the Generations to Come."

This book and all other Destiny Image, Revival Press, Mercy Place, Fresh Bread, Destiny Image Fiction, and Treasure House books are available at Christian bookstores and distributors worldwide.

For a U.S. bookstore nearest you, call 1-800-722-6774.

For more information on foreign distributors, call 717-532-3040.

Reach us on the Internet: www.destinyimage.com.

ISBN 10: 0-7684-2745-2
ISBN 13: 978-0-7684-2745-5

For Worldwide Distribution, Printed in the U.S.A.

1 2 3 4 5 6 7 8 9 10 11 / 13 12 11 10 09

Dedication

I dedicate this book to the queens of my life. To my Mom who gave me life and showed me how to live it. To my wife who made life more amazing than I could imagine. To my new daughter Savannah whose life has brought me so much joy.

Endorsements

Great book! Scot has hit the nail on the head. If you want to become richer and more prosperous, read the words from this great book.

Robert Kiyosaki
Best-selling author of *Rich Dad Poor Dad*

Money is the direct result of how you think and how you act. This book does a great job of teaching you the right way to do both. Read it and heed it!

Larry Winget
New York Times best-selling author of
You're Broke Because You Want To Be

Table of Contents

Foreword

Scot Anderson's *God Wants You Rich* dispels many myths associated with prosperity among God's people. The principles throughout this insightful piece are so simple, they make the book ingenious.

The concepts you'll learn from this book will change your mind about wealth and may assist you to becoming a millionaire if that's your desire. Don't believe me? Just ask more than 150 members of Scot's congregation how they happened to become millionaires after Scot introduced them to new ideas and wealth-creation strategies.

Scot will teach you how to use your talents, abilities, and skills to take your life to unprecedented heights. His message brings passion, hope, and insight, helping people break out of the poverty mindset that holds most of us back.

Besides being an author, pastor, and mentor, Scot is an electrifying speaker, motivating his audiences to *get out of their head and into their greatness*. Being personally inspired by Scot, I find him to be a young man of strong values and vision who is an example of what he articulates.

God Wants You Rich is a reminder that we should *live full and die empty,* recognizing we are made in the likeness and image of God and have been given authority and dominion over everything on the face of the earth, including financial hardship. We showed up rich with love, laughter, talents, and abilities, ready to impact the world, change lives, and dwell in prosperity, happiness, and peace of mind.

God told Abraham, "I'll give you all your eyes can see." Scot helps us open our eyes to see the God-given blessings and opportunities that many of us have overlooked and have yet to maximize.

Set aside time to take in each page as a blueprint to guide you on a successful journey to new riches in relationships, good health, and financial blessings beyond your wildest imagination.

Les Brown

Chapter 1

Would Jesus Hang Around You, or Are You Like a Pharisee?

There are a few things I would like you to do while reading this book. I believe this will greatly increase what you get out of it.

First of all, I want you to ask yourself, "If Jesus were here physically today, would He hang out with me?" I realize this is a weird question. Please follow me through this thought.

I know we have the WWJD bands—"What would Jesus do?" I want the WJHOWM band—"Would Jesus hang out with me?" I believe this thought could be very eye-opening to a lot of Christians out there.

Understand, I'm not talking so much about what you do on the outside, but rather what you believe on the inside. Remember, Jesus had no problem hanging out with the sinners of the day. It was the religious whom He could not stand. It was the Pharisees, the legalistic, the judgmental of the day, those who elevated the rules above what was right, the ones who said, "Hey, you can't heal on the Sabbath." Jesus, of course, knew that the rule doesn't supersede the heart behind the rule. God never intended the rule to keep someone from being healed. That wasn't the purpose of the rule.

The Pharisees were the ones who elevated the rules above the heart of God. They had all the *don'ts* of the Bible, not realizing that the Bible isn't about the *don'ts*, but about the *dos*, not what we can't do and have, but about what we can do and what we can have.

The Pharisees were the ones always looking into what everyone else was doing, but Jesus very clearly said, don't worry about the speck in another's eye, worry about that log in yours (see Luke 6:42). Basically, work on being the best you can be. Don't be upset because the pastor got a new car; worry about you. Don't be so worried about all the sins others are committing; worry about how you can live a better life. You will never win the world through condemnation and judgment. Jesus said we will win the world through love.

Jesus could stand everyone—sinners, prostitutes, thieves—just not Pharisees.

...Now do ye Pharisees make clean the outside of the cup and the platter; but your inward part is full of ravening and wickedness. Ye fools, did not He that made that which is without make that which is within also? But rather give alms of such things as ye have; and, behold, all things are clean unto you. But woe unto you, Pharisees! for ye tithe mint and rue and all manner of herbs, and pass over judgment and the love of God: these ought ye to have done, and not to leave the other undone. Woe unto you, Pharisees! for ye love the uppermost seats in the synagogues, and greetings in the markets. Woe unto you, scribes and Pharisees, hypocrites! for ye are as graves which appear not, and the men that walk over them are not aware of them (Luke 11:39-44 KJV).

This is Jesus speaking. He called them a "brood of vipers" (see Matt. 23:33). It seems that Jesus could not stand them. Why? Because the Pharisees were all about the rules, and forgot about the love of God.

I ask you, then, which are you? Are you all about the rules? Is your life spent judging others or loving others? Are you looking at what others are doing wrong, or are you changing what you are doing wrong?

Are you loving people into the Kingdom, or are you judging them out of it?

My question to you is, are you a sinner like the rest of us, or a religious Pharisee? We know who Jesus will hang out with. My question is, would He hang out with you?

 My question to you is, are you a sinner like the rest of us, or a religious Pharisee?

The next thing I want you to do is read this book with an open mind. When you read this, you will be reading it through one of three different eyes.

Some of you don't know what you believe. You may be a new Christian, or someone who is just interested in this debate. You will get the most out of this book. You come into it with an open mind and an open heart. Of course, from your own experiences, you will draw your own set of beliefs concerning God and success.

Some of you believe God wants you blessed, so you are reading this with a positive outlook, trying to confirm what you believe, looking for answers to the questions some of your friends and acquaintances with different beliefs have. You may even have some of your own questions for which you are seeking answers. This book will really bless you.

Some of you believe God doesn't want everyone blessed, or in some cases, no one blessed. If this is you, you might be reading this book through the eyes of what is wrong with this book. You might even be looking for anything you can twist and turn for a nasty review on amazon.com. (There is a difference between constructive criticism and being judgmental.) You might read this book with a type of anger: "How dare he say things like that?" If you do, you will not see areas in your life that need to change. You will be closed off to anything new. You will be like the Pharisees with Jesus, so set in their old ways, old doctrines, and religion that they could not see the Savior right before their eyes.

> *The lamp of the body is the eye. If therefore your eye is good, your whole body will be full of light. But if your eye is bad, your whole body will be full of darkness. If therefore the light that is in you is darkness, how great is that darkness!* (Matthew 6:22-23)

If you look at this book through an open eye, you will find some light for your life. If you look at it through a judging eye, you will find nothing good.

While reading this book, you may find some controversy rising up inside of you from teachings you heard back in Sunday school. Let's be honest. There are

Scriptures that talk against wealth, and there are Scriptures that talk for wealth. What in the world do you do with that? In the middle of it all, you have the Scripture that says a double-minded man is unstable in all his ways (see James 1:8). There are so many Christians who are unstable in their lives. They want wealth; they want prosperity, but deep down on the inside, they believe money is evil. This double-mindedness is holding them back.

Because of this, I want you to do two things. Number one is what I call the fruit test. Take the teaching or belief and look at what it produces. Does it produce good fruit? Look at the results of the teaching. Does the teaching produce good results? If so, great. If the teaching does not produce good results, then do what Jesus said, and cut it down. Do this with any of your beliefs. I believe it is important to constantly be challenging beliefs—looking at our lives, seeing areas that are not producing, going to the root of them, and seeing what beliefs we need to change.

Number two, ask the question, does the teaching go along with the heart of God? Healing on the Sabbath—yes, that is a good thing. It goes along with the heart of God. The rule is not elevated above loving others.

This question keeps us from legalism, a very dangerous place to be.

Consider this example of legalism: let's say I tell my older son not to get out of bed at night. Let's say he hears a scary noise and fear grips him. A child raised in a legal-istic home would just lie there all night, scared to death. A child raised in a non-legalistic home knows that love supersedes the rule. I would never want my son to lie afraid in bed. I'd tell him to please come get me.

There are Christians today living in a legalistic world, looking down on people because they have tattoos, because they have long hair, because they have been divorced. They take one Scripture, pull it out of the Bible, and build a whole religion against a person. But my Bible says love. Love the sinner, love the divorcée, love the adul-terer, love…

Not healing on the Sabbath was a rule, but it wasn't God's heart. The result was a rule that did not produce good fruit. Jesus cut it down.

 Never elevate the rule above God's heart.

Let me give you a modern example. Some have taken First Corinthians 14:34 out of context and will not allow women to speak in church. Even today I have people coming up to me complaining about women speakers.

But if you go to Galatians, you will read:

There is neither Jew nor Greek, there is neither slave nor free, there is neither male nor female; for you are all one in Christ Jesus (Galatians 3:28).

17

Which is true? Which one produces results that go along with what is best for the Body of Christ?

First, let's look at the religious side. Religion takes First Corinthians 14:34 and creates an entire doctrine out of it, and then will not allow women to speak in church. This basically paralyzes half of the Body of Christ, even though women are just as smart as men, and most of the time know the Word better than we do. That's just a fact. Women read spiritual books and the Bible at a 5 to 1 ratio compared to men. For every one book we read, they read five.

Women bring a female perspective to the Word, a side men miss. Look at what Joyce Meyer has done, at what my mother, Maureen Anderson, has done. Look at the millions of lives that have been touched. Look at the millions of people who have been saved because of their ministries.

Which of the two beliefs do you think produces fruit? Which belief strengthens the Body of Christ? Which one has weakened it for thousands of years? Which belief goes along with the heart of God?

Study that Scripture in First Corinthians, and you'll find that Paul was talking to a specific church where women were out of control. He wasn't talking about all churches for the rest of eternity.

Some churches say that if you have been divorced, you can't be a pastor. I know a guy who made a mistake when he was 19 years old and got divorced within a year. He found Jesus at age 21 and met his wife at 22. They had been married ten years and had a great marriage, but he could not teach above the junior high level because he had been divorced.

Of course, one of the pastors had lived with a girl when he was in college. But I guess as long as he didn't marry her, all was fine. In my view, at least the non-pastor was committed. Do you see how a stupid rule or law can supersede the heart of God? You have a man who could offer so much to the church today, but can't because of man's stupid rules. Isn't God a forgiving God? A Pharisee gets a rule and exalts the rule above love. As I always say, "Let he who has no sin cast the first stone"! (See John 8:7.)

So those who are against wealth have their Scriptures that are against wealth—Scriptures pulled out of context that people have built a whole judgmental religion upon. On the other hand, I have a lot of Scriptures, as you will see, that say God wants you blessed and prosperous. Which is it? In this book, we will go through the fruit test and heart of God test.

I ask that you open up your mind and do your own tests. Pharisees, please read no further! You are wasting your time.

Action Steps

√   Ask yourself, "If Jesus were here physically today, would He hang out with me?" Be sure to answer why or why not.

√   Purpose to have an open mind while reading this book. Ask the Lord to show you any mindsets you may need to change.

√   Think of a teaching you have found controversial in the past. Apply the "fruit test" to it. Does the teaching produce good fruit?

√   Now apply the "heart test" to the teaching you found controversial. Does it go along with the heart of God?

√   Think of a time you may have operated according to a religious rule rather than loving another with the heart of God. If possible, take a step to correct the situation.

Key Points and Personal Adaptions

_____

_____

_____

_____

_____

_____

_____

_____

_____

_____

_____

_____

_____

_____

Chapter 2

Is Money Evil?

In writing a book about wealth, it's important to define what the key issue is. The overall debate is about money. Is money evil?

There are a lot of people screaming out, "Money is evil!" "It is the root of all evil." "Money destroys lives!"

Let's kick over that sacred cow once and for all.

Money is not evil! A hundred dollar bill has no power. I have one in my wallet right now, and if left alone, it would never do anything—good or evil. Money has no power. Do your own test: take some money and leave it alone in a drawer for a month. Then write down all the evil it did.

This money is neither good nor evil. It is amoral, meaning it is not good or evil; it is what is done with money that makes it good or evil.

Take this example: is a baseball bat good or evil? It is neither. It is amoral. If I take my kids outside and play baseball with them, having a great time strengthening my relationship with them, well, the bat has been an instrument of good. If I take the bat and smash my neighbor's car with it, well, the bat has been a tool for evil. It actually isn't the bat that is good or evil, but what I do with the bat.

Is money good or evil? If I take a hundred dollars out and buy time with a hooker, some cocaine, and a Michael Moore DVD, the money has been used for evil (the Michael Moore part is just plain funny...). If I take a hundred dollars and take my family out for a great family night, the money has brought about good.

It isn't the money; it is the person using the money. It is what you do with the money. It is the heart of the individual with the money.

A pastor was given a million dollars by a gangster-type individual who made the money through gambling. The Christian community was outraged by this. "The money is evil!" they cried out.

What a bunch of nuts! Can you honestly say that every dollar in your wallet has always done what was right? How in the heck do you know? The money is not evil. The pastor used the money to further God's ministry. Was the money good or evil? Neither, but it produced good. I also read that the wealth of the wicked is laid up for the just (see Prov. 13:22). What kind of crazy Christian wants to give the wealth back to the wicked?

"Well, Pastor, I know some people who got money, and it destroyed their lives. Thus money is evil."

Well, I know some people who got married, and it destroyed their lives. Under that same thinking, I have to assume that marriage is evil. Makes no sense, does it? I know a lot more people who lost all their money, and it destroyed them. But wait a minute. I thought you said not having money was a good thing?

Those whose lives were destroyed didn't have a good foundation. They were not ready for the money. Or they were not ready for marriage.

 If you don't have a good foundation, just about anything can destroy your life.

The Bible says to build your house on the rock, on the Word. When we live a life in the Word, growing and changing, then things in life cannot destroy our lives. Having money or losing money cannot destroy my life. It is not the money that destroyed these people, but rather what was inside them.

They didn't have self-control. They lacked character. They didn't understand that relationships are the most important thing in life. Jesus said, "I can sum the whole Bible up in this one statement: Love God; love others as yourself" (see Luke 10:27). Life is about relationships. It is about your relationship with God, with others, and with yourself. If you make those relationships a priority, neither money nor anything else can destroy your life. If I love God, I could never do anything to hurt His heart. I can't go out and feed the flesh. If I love my wife, I can't do anything that would destroy my marriage. If I love myself, I can't do anything that destroys this temple.

"Pastor, I know men who have money, and they left their wives and kids."

I know a lot more men who had no money and did the same. It had nothing to do with the money; it had everything to do with what was in them. I know plenty of men who have come into wealth, myself included, and it made marriage a lot easier.

"They say that 75 percent of divorces are because of finances. Most fights are about money."

The pressure that a lack of money creates often causes what is inside of us to come to the surface—fears, anger, unbelief—which puts additional stress on our relationships. If lack is more spiritual, then why in the heck does it cause more fights? Men, you have never said to your wives, "Hey! You just aren't spending enough money. If you want this marriage to work, you better get off your backside and start spending." Women, you have never said to your husbands, "You are making way too much money. Knock it off!"

Lack of money has been a contributing factor to a lot more divorces than too much money. There is a major flaw in the statement that money contributes to divorce. It is a lack of money.

"OK, Pastor Scot, what about where Jesus said it is easier for a camel to go through the eye of needle than it is for a rich man to enter into the Kingdom of God"? (see Matt. 19:24).

I believe this is true. If you take what we call a self-made millionaire, and try to get him saved, it is very difficult. He has done it on his own. He feels like he doesn't need God. Though there is an emptiness inside of him that he tries to fill with another drink, or with another conquest, some more drugs, a bigger boat, another marriage, he doesn't realize that the only way he can fill that void is through a relationship with God. God doesn't make sense to him. He has the I-can-do-it-on-my-own mentality. It is very hard to get him saved.

But for the man (or woman) who was saved and just getting by, who started applying biblical principles to his finances, and then became a millionaire, you could never get him out of Christianity. He feels like he could not have done it without God. As the world would say, he got his cake and got to eat it, too. He got the money, and more importantly, the relationship with his Daddy. To him, it couldn't have been done without God.

Since we have started teaching this in our church, nearly 150 people have become millionaires. I don't know any of them who had a good relationship with God before the money, who don't have an even stronger relationship with Him today.

So someone unsaved with lots of money has a hard time getting into the Kingdom. (It's possible though—even Jesus said that in the next verse.) But someone who is saved and then experiences the blessings is hard to get out of the Kingdom.

Other statements are thrown out there like, "Well, the Bible says that money is the root of all evil."

I always ask, "Where in the Bible does it say that?" I have never been able to find that Scripture.

Isn't it funny how a Scripture taken and taught out of context can impact the thinking of a generation? I find it even sadder that people take what they hear to be true without really getting into the Word and finding out if it is true. Just because a pastor says something does not make it true. You are responsible to research what is said.

I had a friend who was moving to Arizona. He got himself a realtor and began looking for a house. He really wanted a house with a pool, but the realtor, for reasons only known to God, kept taking him to houses without a pool—which in Arizona is not the best idea. My friend came home and said, "Is it true that people in Arizona are no longer putting in pools, and that most people are filling their pools up with dirt?"

I said, "That lacks all common sense. I promise you that is not true."

We look at that and say, "Yes, that lacks common sense and is not true." But a guy in a suit tells you that money is evil, and you say, "Oh, that makes perfect sense." Actually it makes no sense. Research it.

The Bible, in First Timothy 6:10, says, "The love of money is the root of all evil" (KJV).

There is a huge difference. Yes, the love of money is wrong. Now, I do like money a lot, but love, probably not. This passage is admonishing us not to elevate money above what is really important in life. Don't elevate money above your marriage, above your children, above your relationship with God. Money becomes the root of all evil when it becomes more important than God, more important than people. When you love money and cannot give it away or bless others with it, then it has become a problem.

When I go into business with people, I always let them know that money is not as important as our relationship. I have had people rip me off. Did it make me upset? (Honestly, of course, I was initially mad.) But I have to remind myself that relationships are more important than money. I forgive and move on. I just look at it like I blessed them with some money. I guard my heart, and I make sure that my values stay in order.

Loving money is wrong, but there is nothing wrong with wanting financial security so you no longer have to worry about losing the house or keeping the electricity on. What is wrong with having such financial blessings that you now become the financial blessing in other people's lives?

Do you know what is better than the financial miracle of someone giving you the $500 you need for rent? Never needing a miracle. What is even better than that is the moment you become the miracle in someone else's life.

Many have said, "Having too much money is evil." OK, what is too much? Who determines this magical number? Remember, all you Americans out there, that in most third world countries, $1 a day is a lot of money. So does that mean if you make more than a $1 a day you have too much money? Does that mean that third world countries are more spiritual than we are? Is that homeless guy on the street living God's dream for his life?

Does it mean that having more than $5 in the bank is evil? Who gets to be the evil police today? What Pharisee wants to be the judge? A poor person in America is a wealthy person in a lot of countries today. Does that make you evil? If you make over $5,000 a year are you living in sin?

This thinking is too inconsistent. You have to go to the Word. "Don't judge." I love that. Don't worry about how much money other people have, or what they are doing with their money. You worry about you. Don't worry about what kind of car others are driving. And stop using the phrase, "Well, they should give that money to the poor." What did Jesus say when someone was dumping perfume on His feet that was worth one year's salary—in today's numbers more than $40,000—and someone said it should be given to the poor? Jesus said, "The poor you will have with you always" (see Matt. 26:11). Jesus said it, not me. Come on, how many times have you heard someone say that! Over 2,000 years later and Christians are still saying the same judgmental thing.

Once again, get out of your holier-than-thou attitude. Stop judging others and live your own life. I give more away in a year than poverty-minded Christians can give away in a lifetime. I still drive a Hummer, live in a very nice house, and have probably too many big screen televisions. But in the grand scheme of life, because I am blessed, I can give out of my abundance.

Here are some amazing Scriptures on enjoying what God has given you. I want you to think about your blessings as if they are from a good Dad, a great God. What dad doesn't want his kids to enjoy what he has given them? I love the Christmas holidays and watching my kids with all their gifts, seeing them enjoying the blessings I have given to them. In the same sense, I enjoy this with them because they are kids who love to give to others. They have no problem sharing and giving. Once again, it comes down to their heart. I love for them to enjoy life and all life has to offer. My condition is that their heart is right. I believe the same is true for God.

Here is what I have seen: It is good and fitting for one to eat and drink, and to enjoy the good of all his labor in which he toils under the sun all the days of his life which God gives him; for it is his heritage. As for every man to whom God has given riches and wealth, and given him power to eat of it, to receive his heritage and rejoice in his labor—this is the gift of God. For he will not dwell unduly on the days of his life, because God keeps him busy with the joy of his heart (Ecclesiastes 5:18-20).

God says to enjoy the good of all your labor. God gives us riches and wealth, and wants us to eat from them. There is nothing wrong with me enjoying my amazing home, my Hummer, my awesome pool, my great vacations at the Cape. God wants me to enjoy these things just like I want my kids to enjoy their blessings. But it is about my heart. Do I love others? Do I give? Am I blessed to be a blessing?

Here is a great story. As I have said, I am a good and giving father. I took my kids out for a movie one day. Before we went in, I allowed each child to pick out the candy he wanted. Laken wanted licorice, Heath wanted Dots, Baylor wanted a candy bar, and Peyton, my youngest, wanted Dad's favorite, Gummi Bears.

In my mind, I was thinking, *I will just have some of each child's candy. Why buy more? I will have a smorgasbord of candy.*

We got the candy and went into the movie. I leaned over to Laken and said, "Let me have some licorice."

Laken replied, "Sure, Dad," and gave me a handful of licorice.

The same thing happened with Baylor and with Heath.

Then came the time for Peyton. I leaned over and said, "Peyton, let Dad have some Gummies."

He pulled his candy away, and said, "Dad, these are mine!"

This shocked me. I sat there thinking, *you are sitting there in the clothes I have provided for you. You rode here in the car I paid for. You have the food in your belly from lunch that I paid for. You are sitting here in the movie I paid for, eating the Gummies I provided, and you tell me to get my own.* (I took care of that little scenario.)

At that point, do I, as his father, feel like blessing him, giving to him? Absolutely not. My heart is a reflection of his. When you and I get into, "This is my money. Sorry, God, I don't believe in the tithe. I work hard for this money. It's mine," I wonder if God's heart mirrors ours. We wonder why the blessings aren't coming our way.

God wants us to enjoy our stuff, but He wants us to always have a giving heart.

> *If a man begets a hundred children and lives many years, so that the days of his years are many, but his soul is not satisfied with goodness* [original translation: cannot enjoy his prosperity], *or indeed he has no burial, I say that a stillborn child is better than he* (Ecclesiastes 6:3).

What a waste of life if you don't enjoy it. God wants you to enjoy life and all the good things of life.

 Stop making judgmental comments, and start living life.

Even if you don't agree with this, please remember the Bible says don't judge. That means don't judge me and my Hummer, me and my nice house. I enjoy life, I love life, and I believe this pleases God.

Here is an amazing Scripture. I will let you do what you want with it.

A feast is made for laughter, and wine makes merry; but money answers everything (Ecclesiastes 10:19).

We need to send Bibles to India. Money answers that.

We need food for those starving in Africa. Money answers that.

We have single moms who are homeless. Money answers that.

I don't have time to volunteer at the church. Money answers that.

I don't have money to give to the church. Money answers that.

We have a dying world that needs to hear the Gospel. Money answers that.

And God is able to make all grace abound toward you, that you, always having all sufficiency in all things, may have an abundance for every good work (2 Corinthians 9:8).

"Wait a minute. I am supposed to have what? An abundance? Not just enough? Not struggling? I thought I was supposed to be broke and just making it to be spiritual."

Poverty-minded Christians give a little out of their lack. I am able to give a lot out of my abundance. Don't judge me in my nice suit, my nice car, and my nice house.

Don't get mad at this statement, but it is true. Being poor and staying poor in the name of spirituality is one of the most selfish things you can do.

 Yes, I said it. If this is how you live, you are all about you and your spirituality. "Look at *me*; look at what *I* give up; look at how *I* suffer." You have everything pointing to you.

But wait. I thought that all we do is to point to Jesus. For my life, I say, "Look at what *God* has done. Look at what *God* can do for you." If you believe it is spiritual to be poor, your poor life is all about what *you* do. My life is about what *God* does. Not just that, but look at the millions of lives I am able to touch with my abundance.

Action Steps

√ Set aside time today to build your personal relationship with God.

√ Make a plan to spend quality time with your family, or a good friend, this week.

√ Has someone ripped you off? If so, take some time right now to forgive them and then purpose to move on.

√ What blessings has God, as your loving Father, given you recently? Count them.

√ Make a list of needs in the world or the Church that you would like to help meet, if you had enough money.

Key points and personal adaption

_____

_____

_____

_____

_____

_____

_____

_____

_____

_____

_____

_____

_____

_____

Chapter 3

The Purpose of Money

Whether you are for or against money, you still need it. That is a fact. When it's time to pay rent, the time you've spent in prayer does not get credited to your bill. The number of people you have led to salvation does not help pay the electric bill. You need money. It is what buys Bibles, sends people on missionary trips, builds churches, pays bills, buys food...

We need money individually. But from a Body of Christ perspective, we really need money, and we need lots of it.

If we want to send Bibles to China, what do we need? Money.

If we want to feed the homeless, what do we need? Money.

If we want to send missionaries to Africa, what do we need? Money.

If we want to reach more people through radio and television, what do we need? Money.

To touch the world with the Gospel, what do we need? Money.

The more money we have, the faster and more efficiently we can do these things. If the wealth of the wicked was in the hands of the just, reaching people for Jesus would be a simple thing. Based on that, what do you suppose God thinks about His kids having money?

Most Christians remain in the "just get by" state because deep down they have a misconception that it is spiritual to be poor. It is this battle within you that keeps you there. Many of you who are Christians want abundance; you want to change, but as you think, so are you. Jesus said that out of the abundance of your heart you bring forth your life (see Luke 6:45). If poverty is in you, guess what will come out of you? If "just get by" is in you, guess what comes out of you?

Deep down inside of you, in the subconscious area, is your belief system. (I really get into this in my books *Think Like a Billionaire, Become a Billionaire,* and *Millionaire Habits in 21 Days.* Both can be found at www.lifewithscot.com.) For now, a quick overview. It is this belief system that makes 95 percent of your decisions throughout the day. It determined how you responded to your wife when she came home. You didn't think it through (obviously, or you wouldn't be fighting right now). It just came out of you. Someone cuts you off in traffic. You didn't think through giving them the one finger peace sign. It just happened. It came out of you.

What you believe acts like a homing device. It will take you right to what you expect out of life.

 If you think it is spiritual to be poor, you will be poor.

So it stays away from good opportunities, keeps you away from anything that could bring wealth into your life. You may want wealth, but in areas deep down that you have not dealt with, you still have a problem with money. We need to uproot those beliefs.

Until you change that area of thinking, you will be stuck just getting by.

The biggest problem that holds the Church back from doing so much more, the problem that keeps the wealth of the wicked in the hands of the wicked, is this thought that has been passed down from generation to generation. It is the thought that it is spiritual to be poor.

We have this belief inside of us, and if we can't change that foundational belief, then we will never step into abundance. Where you are inside is where you are going to be outside. As long as you think it is wrong to have money, you won't. Until you can break that one thought, you will never be able to step into the abundance that God wants you to have.

I was recently in Rome and visited Vatican City. This priceless facility is worth trillions of dollars, yet it sends out the message that it is spiritual to be poor. It contains millions of square feet, yet the pope, the biggest religious leader of the day, lives in a humble 800-square foot apartment.

I told my dad, "Make me pope. I will change the world in one day. All I have to do is make two little changes. One, the pope is getting married. I'm no good leading the church with all this testosterone flowing through my veins. Number two, I'm taking over one of these buildings as my home."

All of a sudden, the message that it is all right to have abundance, that being poor isn't spiritual, will begin to permeate the Body of Christ. All of a sudden, you will have Christians out getting the wealth that was laid up for them. All of sudden, it will be a benefit to be a Christian, not a burden. In two acts, I could literally change the world, this generation, and many generations to come.

I really want you to understand this next statement:

From cover to cover, the Bible is all about being blessed so that we can be a blessing.

Look at how Paul said it:

For you know the grace of our Lord Jesus Christ, that though He was rich, yet for your sakes He became poor, that you through His poverty might become rich (2 Corinthians 8:9).

And he continues in the next chapter:

And God is able to make all grace abound toward you, that you, always having all sufficiency in all things, [this last part is what it is all about] *may have an abundance for every good work* (2 Corinthians 9:8).

If I have just enough, God is unable to say, "Hey, give over here, give over there." I can't give out of my lack. But if I have this abundance He is talking about, I can give for every good work.

Right now, if you heard they needed Bibles in India, could you give them $250,000 for Bibles? Most of us could give a few hundred dollars. That still is a huge stretch for many Christians today. Imagine if you could say, "How many Bibles do you need? Will a million do? Let me write you a check." You have positioned yourself to be a blessing. You are blessed to be a blessing. You can give out of your abundance, not your lack!

That is the purpose of money! Being blessed to be a blessing.

In Genesis 12:2-3, God said to Abraham, "I will make you average; you will struggle financially; you will live paycheck to paycheck." Oh, wait a second, it doesn't say that. That is out of the ISTBP version (It's Spiritual To Be Poor Version). My Bible says, "I will make you a mighty nation. I will make you abundant. I am going to make you blessed so that you can be a blessing." Right there. Did you catch it? That is God's plan.

He wants you blessed so you can be a blessing. Imagine if your church was filled with millionaires and billionaires. The church has a building fund. It needs $10 million. Seven people stand up and say, "It is covered. Move on." The church wants to send Bibles to India. "Will a million dollars cover it?" Look at what the Church can do when the wealth is in our hands.

My goal is for that Scripture to become past tense for this generation (see Prov. 13:22). No longer will the wealth of the wicked be laid up for the just; it will be in the hands of the just.

How in the world can anyone argue with that? Look at what the Body of Christ could do if we had the money.

The world would begin to turn to us for help. If another Hurricane Katrina happens, the whole world turns to the Church, and we say, "We got it. How much do you need? Will $100 billion do? Do you need more? Just let us know. Who do we make the check out to? We can handle it because we are so blessed."

Imagine what you could do with the $60 billion that Bill Gates has. You could pay off every single church in America. You could provide Bibles for everyone in the world.

 Imagine what the Body of Christ could do if we controlled the wealth. We could do what we were called to do: *change the world.*

Once again, do you see how the teaching that God wants you poor makes no sense? It limits what we can do. It holds us back.

It actually keeps people from living the life God has for them. It keeps them from fulfilling their God-given purpose.

Most people don't get into their God-given purpose, not because they don't want to, not because they don't have a desire to, not because they haven't read *The Purpose Driven Life*, but because they have to spend all their time and energy working for their money.

We have become slaves to money. Most people have to work 40, 50, 60 hours a week for their money. That is just to live. Your money controls your life. You don't have the time to do what God has called you to do. You can't go to Africa on the missions trip that God put on your heart because you don't have the money, and you can't take the time off. You can't give like you want to give. You can't spend the time you want to spend on your purpose.

A lot of Christians spend a lifetime being slaves to money, all in the name of being spiritual.

Now, imagine if you learned how to invest. Instead of burying your talent, you learned how to make your talent produce. God then gives you more talents. He produces more in your life. All of a sudden you wake up one day, and your money is working for you.

Now you have 40, 50, 60 hours to give into the Kingdom to be a blessing. That is time that can go toward your destiny. You can pay for the missions trip, pay for the Bibles. You are blessed to be a blessing. You have lived a life that has benefited the Body of Christ.

How in the world can anyone argue against that?

If we follow God's plan, we can get to the place where we say, "OK, Church, I've got forty hours. What do you need me to do? I can help out and do whatever you need because I've got the money working for me."

Rather than putting in 40 hours working so my worldly boss can become rich, I am rich, and my money is working so I can further the Kingdom of God.

It is time that this wealth gets into our hands. The world has no clue what to do with it. They waste it on drugs and alcohol and a myriad of other things, trying to find some peace, trying to find some happiness. The Bible asks, what good is it to gain the whole world but lose your soul? (See Matthew 16:26.) You lose your ability to be happy. The Bible says God gave the Israelites the desires of their hearts but sent leanness to their souls (see Ps. 106:15). They lost the ability to be happy. You can get rich the world's way. People do it all the time. But they have no peace, no joy, no happiness.

This book is about doing it God's way. God's way is to have a heart and attitude of giving. We are blessed so we can be a blessing on all occasions. In a sense, I get my cake, and I eat it, too, because I have the abundance. But more importantly, I also have happiness, peace, and joy.

The world is confused about what to do with their money. It makes me laugh when I see big Hollywood concerts that they put on to raise money for AIDS or some other charity. They get 15 bands together (who are just doing it for positive publicity), and they do a big concert and raise $300,000. I watch this, thinking, "You made over $30 million last year. If you just gave your tithe of $3 million dollars, we would have ten times the money and wouldn't have to watch your stupid concert. We wouldn't have to listen to how concerned you are. If you're concerned, give out of your abundance."

Imagine if each artist at the concert, each producer, and each movie star gave. They could hand over a check for $30 billion. That would take care of world hunger for a decade. But the world doesn't know what to do with its money.

The young generation is looking to the celebrities and saying, "I want to be like Brad Pitt," or, "I want to be like Julia Roberts." My goal in my generation is for the Body of Christ to get to the place where the young generation wants to be like us. They say, "I want to be like that man of God." "I want to be like that woman of God."

I want a new television show. Instead of *Lifestyles of the Rich and Famous*, I want *Lifestyles of the Rich and Christian*. Now that would be a television show where we are blessed and we are pouring out the blessings.

Action Steps

√   Determine in your heart that God wants to bless you so you can be a blessing. Remind yourself of that every day this week.

√   Find a way to use what you have already been blessed with to bless someone in need.

√   Begin to dream about what you will do to change the world as God helps you gain additional resources.

√   Imagine your church is featured on *Lifestyles of the Rich and Christian*. What could happen on this episode?

Key points and personal adaption

_____

_____

_____

_____

_____

_____

_____

_____

_____

_____

_____

_____

_____

_____

Chapter 4

God Filled the Pantry;
Now Make Some Breakfast.

Deuteronomy 8:18 says God gives you "power to get wealth." Now why would God *give* you the power to get wealth, *tell* you that He gave you the power, and then *get mad* at you for using the power? That doesn't make any sense at all.

Let me give you an example. I, of course, am the daddy to my four boys. In my house, I have a pantry full of great things for breakfast. I have provided for them all the cereal their little hearts could desire. There are Pop-Tarts. There are granola bars. We have eggs, bacon, and ham in the fridge. In the freezer I have laid up some Eggos if they choose. I have told them, "You have the power to obtain your breakfast." The breakfast of the pantry is laid up for my children.

Let's say on Saturday, Dad gets up and comes downstairs at 9:00 A.M. (kind of early for me, but it could happen). At the foot of the stairs is my eldest son, Laken. He cries out to me, "Abba, Father, why have you forsaken me? Where is thine breakfast you have spake unto me? Have you not heard my cries for breakfast? I thought surely the windows of Heaven would open up and breakfast would overflow me. Were you teaching thine lesson to me? Were you humbling me through this tribulation of hunger?"

I say, "Uhmmmm, no. None of the above. I provided for you all you needed for breakfast. I even gave you permission to have breakfast. I laid up the breakfast for you. All you had to do was get it."

Would it make sense for me as a father to provide the breakfast, give my children the power to get breakfast, and then get mad at them for making breakfast? Of course not. That makes no sense.

I want the Body of Christ to get this. God gave you the power to get wealth. He has even laid up the wealth for you. He said "laid up," not "dropped in your lap." Laid up means you have to go get it. You have to start a business, invent an product, open a restaurant, put your hands to something He can bless. God has placed you—even in the midst of an economic downturn—in the greatest time of wealth the world has ever known. He says, "Go get it. Stop whining about it; go get it."

And please don't be the kid who comes upstairs whining, "Dad, Laken is making breakfast, and he made too big of a bowl of cereal for himself. Daddy, it is evil for him to have too much."

I would say, "Son, there is more than enough for all of you to have too much. I am a too-much daddy. Stop worrying about what others get. Nobody likes a tattletale. Go enjoy the blessings I have set before you."

God gave you the power. He wants you to use the power so that you can be blessed to be a blessing. He says, "Go make your breakfast. I have set it before you."

I like what Deuteronomy 30:19 says:

I call heaven and earth as witnesses today against you, that I have set before you life and death, blessing and cursing; therefore choose life, that both you and your descendants may live.

It is a multiple choice test. Life or death, blessings or curses. But He gives you a hint. "Pssst. Choose life." I ask you, why in the world are so many Christians choosing poverty?

Come on, Church, let's choose life. Let's choose abundance. Let's choose to go into all God has laid out for us and get our hands on that breakfast.

We live in the pantry of life. God has given everyone reading this book the opportunity and the resources for great wealth.

 In America we have the greatest opportunity that the world has ever known for wealth and abundance. All God is saying is go get it.

The Bible says the wealth of the wicked is laid up for the just. Number one, He wouldn't lay it up for us if He didn't want us to have it. Number two, it is laid up. The Bible doesn't say it is dropped in the laps of the just. It says "laid up," meaning we have to go get it.

It is time Christians went out and got what is rightfully theirs. It is time we got the money from the world and started using it the way God intended, to be a blessing on all occasions.

Action Steps

√   Take inventory of your "pantry." What has God laid up for you that you can use to get wealth?

√   Decide to take one of your dreams off "hold"—will you pursue an invention, start a business, finish your degree? Write out the steps needed to finalize that goal.

√   Choose life!

Key points and personal adaption

_____

_____

_____

_____

_____

_____

_____

_____

_____

_____

_____

_____

_____

_____

_____

Chapter 5

Stop Making God Small and Insignificant; No One Wants to Be On a Losing Team.

 Let them shout for joy and be glad, Who favor My righteous cause; And let them say continually, "Let the Lord be magnified, Who has pleasure in the prosperity of His servant" (Psalm 35:27).

What a sick God we would serve if He took pleasure in our prosperity and then was angry at us for having it. God can't be happy and angry at the same time. I like the part of this Scripture that says God takes pleasure in our prosperity, but let's not overlook this key statement:

Let the Lord be magnified.

Understand that our prosperity is to magnify the Lord. In other words, it is to make God look bigger to the world. It is the same meaning as "glorify God." When you glorify Him, you make Him bigger.

The world, whether you know it or not, is watching you. Your neighbors know that you're a Christian whether you told them or not. They know on Sundays whether you go to church or not. They are looking at your life, your marriage, your children, your finances. They are watching to see if life is different when you are a Christian.

When they look at you and your life is just as broken as theirs, when your marriage is failing just like theirs, when you are having just as much trouble with your kids as they do with theirs, when they see that you are just as broke as they are, they say to themselves, "Why in the world would I want to be a Christian? I have the same things they have except I get to go to the lake on Sunday, and I get to use 10 percent more of my check."

In that scenario, you made God smaller. God became something they didn't need. No condemnation if that is you. I'm just suggesting that we change that.

But it's a whole different story if your neighbors look at you and say, "Why do you have such an amazing life? Why do you have such a great marriage? Your children actually listen to you. You seem to have an abundance in every area of life. We make the same amount of money, and you have so much more in your life. What do you have that we don't have?"

You are able to say, "We have Jesus Christ." Right then you have made God bigger. You have just magnified Him to the world. You did more for the Body of Christ than if you stood on the street corner and preached damnation for 50 years. Your abundant life will get more people saved than a million "You're going to hell! Burn, baby, burn" tracts.

If you are a salesman and you get all the good deals and everything seems to go your way, then you just say, "I've got Jesus Christ." You have just made God bigger.

> ...abstain from fleshly lusts which war against the soul, having your conduct honorable among the Gentiles, that when they speak against you as evildoers, they may, by your good works which they observe, **glorify God** in the day of visitation.

> Therefore submit yourselves to every ordinance of man for the Lord's sake, whether to the king as supreme, or to governors, as to those who are sent by Him for the punishment of evildoers and for the praise of those who do good. For this is the will of God, **that by doing good you may put to silence the ignorance of foolish men**—as free, yet not

*using liberty as a cloak for vice, but as bondservants of God. **Honor all people. Love the brotherhood.** Fear God. Honor the king* (1 Peter 2:11-17).

Basically, don't be judgmental. Don't condemn the world. Stop being a Pharisee. Love the world. Let them look into your life and say, "I want that. I want to be part of that family."

If you're broke, sick, and just getting by, no one wants to be a part of that. They can have that on their own, and they get to stay home on Sundays.

Let me give you an example. My kids obviously are Andersons. They represent Holly and me, and the Anderson family. When they go to school, the teachers, the kids, and the school staff all judge Holly and me not on the truth of who we are, but on our kids' example. That makes sense, right?

The teachers and kids don't know us. They don't know anything about us. They form their opinions of us based on the example of our children. They judge Holly and me based on them.

Let's say we are trying to get people to join the Anderson family at school. My kids, though I have laid up lunch money for them, don't get lunch, and then tell everyone that it is spiritual to skip lunch. "My parents want me poor and hungry," they say, though that is not true, and not my heart at all. How many kids on that day are joining the Anderson family?

Let's say at recess they scream out on the playground that all the other kids will burn if they do not join the Anderson family. They look like a couple of fruitcakes on the playground, not only embarrassing themselves, but also the Anderson name. They picket the new Harry Potter movie, telling the kids how evil they are to watch it. How many Andersons did we get on that day?

What if they told all the kids how I killed their dog and took him away? "Dad needed the dog dead." (An extreme example to show how stupid it is when a pastor tells a child that God took his mommy from him because He needed her in Heaven. How can that be good? When that happens, the child grows up hating any God who would take a mom away from a child.) How many Andersons today?

What if my kids told everyone how, when they were playing in the street, I called up my friend, and had him get in his car and run over them to teach them a lesson? (Once again, an example of how people say God sends punishment to get people. I would never send a car to hit my kids. But if they were not listening and got hit by a car, it would be because they were not following my instructions. Big difference. Yes, there are consequences to sin, but God didn't send them. If you cheat on your wife, God does not send the divorce. The divorce is the consequence of your sin.) How many Andersons today?

What if my kids went to school and told everyone I made them sick that day to teach them a lesson in humility? Great testimony, guys. How many joining up today? None.

What if my kids went to school richly blessed? What if they helped other kids out who didn't have lunch money, and gave out of their abundance? What if they walked in love and not in judgment and seemed to be kind to all the other kids? They were true Andersons that day. How many Andersons do we get now? Far more than we would the other way.

In the same sense, we are God's children. We go out on the playground of life every day. We want people to join our family. No one wants to be on the losing team.

Who wants to be part of something that looks like it is losing? Do you remember in grade school playing soccer, football, kickball, or whatever sport at recess? You started off with equal teams, but in about five minutes, it was 37 kids versus 5. Most of the kids switched to the team that seemed to be doing better. We are struggling to get people to come to church, to join our team. Why? Because no sane person wants to be part of something that trumpets poverty and misery all for the name of Jesus.

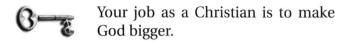 Your job as a Christian is to make God bigger.

I want the world to look into our lives and say, "That is an amazing God they serve, One who takes pleasure in the prosperity of His servants."

You are called to be blessed so you can be a blessing.

It is time we got rid of the religious idea that poverty is spiritual. We need to begin to think the way God thinks and step into the abundance He wants us to have. It is time we allow Him to take pleasure in our prosperity. It is time the Body of Christ got back that which the devil stole. It is time we got that wealth and used it to glorify and magnify God. It is time the world looked at us and said, "I want to be a part of that."

Action Steps

√   Think of a judgment you have held about a person
    or a group of people. Now let that judgment go and
    purpose to walk in love toward them.

√   Ask yourself: "Do I glorify God? Do I make Him
    look bigger? Or do those around me say, 'I don't
    want any part of that family'?" If it is the latter, what
    do you need to change in you so you begin to make
    God look bigger?

√   Pick one thing you can change this week about how
    you live your life in order to make God bigger to
    those around you.

Key points and personal adaption

Chapter 6

What You Expect You Always Get!

It doesn't matter if you are a Christian, a muslim, or a psychologist, most people agree that what you expect out of life you get. The life you are living right now is no more than the substance of what you have expected. If you want to change your life, then you have to raise your expectation. In this chapter I will show you not just what the Bible has been saying about raising your expectations, but what the consensus of psychologists are saying is the only known method of raising expectations. (Of course, this method has been in the Bible for thousands of years, though the world has just discovered it). I believe that this will be the most life-changing chapter in this book. This chapter will help you take your life from just enough, to more than you can contain. And that means your blessings spill over to all those around you.

Hebrews 11:1 says faith is the substance of things *hoped* for. We can agree that the key ingredient in faith is hope. Hope is what produces our substance.

Now the word *hope* does not mean what most Christians today think it means. A wrong definition of hope greatly limits our substance.

To most Christians, that word *hope* means *wish*. You ask a man about his marriage, and he might say something like, "Our marriage is in some trouble; I really hope it gets better." Ask a woman about the economy, and she might say something like, "I hope it gets better. Layoffs are coming; I hope I don't get laid off." Or, hey, how are your kids? "I hope they start listening to me." Do you see that, for many of us, hope is the expression of a wish or a desire? "I wish my kids would listen…I don't want to be laid off…I want my marriage to get better, but who knows?"

That is not hope. Look *hope* up in the dictionary. Hope means to confidently expect something different and favorable. The statements above are not confident; they don't expect change. They don't expect the economy or the marriage to change. They want it or wish it. But faith is not the substance of what you halfheartedly wish for; faith is the substance of what you expect.

You may want a great day tomorrow, but you don't expect it. Your mom never had many great days, nor did your grandparents. Why should you have anything different? So you expect another bad day. Guess what? You get exactly what you expect. Faith is the substance of your expectation for another bad day.

You may want wealth, but finances never worked out for your parents, and have never worked out for you. Deep down you expect to just get by. And you continue to just get by. Faith is the substance of your expectation for just enough.

Expectation has to do with what you think you can have—not what you want, but what you can have. Most Christians don't fully believe that they alone are responsible for the limitations in their lives. You are a child of the King. The Bible says you are a joint heir with Christ Jesus. That means that what is His is yours. You are a prince or princess. You are royalty. You can have wealth; you can have happiness, peace, joy, a long, healthy, prosperous life. These are the promises of God. But if you don't believe you can have them, you won't expect them. Because of this, you will continue to accept far less than you deserve.

This takes me to the major point of this book:

 If you have the misconception that it is more spiritual to be poor, then your expectations for what God can do financially in your life will be greatly limited.

Why would God help you get something He is against?

This brings me to an important point: what you hope for not only determines what you get, but also what you will accept. Let me give you an example.

Peyton is my six-year-old. He has a friend named Drew. Now Drew is one of the most polite kids I have ever met. He reminds me of Eddie Haskel on the "Leave it to Beaver" show. Drew comes over, and I say, "Hi, Drew." He responds with "Hi, Mr. Anderson, thank you so much for allowing me to come over to your beautiful home." Then it is a night of politeness: "Mr. Anderson, if it is not too much trouble, may I please have a drink of water?…Oh, Mr. Anderson, this is the best water I have ever had."

So Peyton and Drew are playing, and Peyton notices that Dad has in his hand some "Nerds" candy (the greatest candy ever made). Peyton cries out, "Dad, can we please have some nerds?" I say, "Yes, come over, boys, and let me give you some candy." Drew is first, and I open the huge box of nerds and drop a single nerd into his hand. (This is my little joke that I do with kids.) Drew's face goes from excitement to frustration to controlled politeness, and he looks up at me and says, "Thank you very much, Mr. Anderson." And he walks away. Peyton comes over, and I do the same thing, I drop a single nerds candy into his outreached hands. Peyton looks at it and cries out, "Daaaaad!!!! Come on!!!!" I say, "Oh sorry, son, is that too much? You want me to cut it in half?" Peyton cries out, "Daaaaad! Stop it.... You give me some nerds!!!!" So I dump a bunch of nerds in his hands. I now turn to Drew and say, "Come get some more nerds." Drew responds, "No, thank you, Mr. Anderson. I have more than enough, I think this will fill me up." "Stop it, Drew, get over here and get your nerds," I say.

Get this. Peyton, who is a child of the candy king, can have a big handful of candy. That is his right. He expects it. Because of his expectation, he does not accept anything less. Drew, on the other hand, has low expectations. He doesn't know what is afforded to him; because of this, he accepts his single nerd candy.

Many Christians out there accept a pittance in their finances, a pittance in their relationships, in their lives. Those who know what life should be, and expect it, are the ones who say, "Daaaaad! Stop, where are my blessings!!!"

A few months ago while walking down the hall, I came upon a pool of water. I noticed that coming from my ceiling was a fountain-like drip of water. I, being a man, fixed it by putting a bowl under it. Holly and I decided to go down and watch a movie. I went to turn on my 65" blessing from God, but it would not turn on. Fine, I went to turn on my projector and watch the movie in the movie room. Same thing, the projector bulb is burned out. OK, let's watch it upstairs in bed. The DVD player in the bedroom would not play the movie. As I was ripping the DVD player off the shelf, planning on tossing it off the balcony, I stopped and said, "God, this is not acceptable. I am a tither and a giver; You protect my stuff. I am owed seven times what has been lost. Take care of it, God." (See Proverbs 6:30-31.)

The insurance agent comes out and says, "I know you can fix the leak for less, but here is $6000. Keep whatever you don't spend." I have the leak and all fixed for $600. I fix the TV and projector for $200, and there you have it, my seven-fold.

That is my life. I do not accept anything that is below my expectations. Many Christians in life just take it. They take that one piece of candy and think it is their lot in life. No, you were created, in the likeness and image of God, to have dominion, to be blessed, to have a great life. As Jesus said, "I came that they may have life, and have it abundantly" (John 10:10).

"Scot, you can't demand like that." Really! Here is Jesus talking about prayer:

 Which of you shall have a friend, and go to him at midnight and say to him, "Friend, lend me three loaves; for a friend of mine has come to me on his journey, and I have nothing to set before him"; and he will answer from within and say, "Do not trouble me; the door is now shut, and my children are with me in bed; I cannot rise and give to you"? I say to you, though he will not rise and give to him because he is his friend, yet because of his persistence he will rise and give him as many as he needs.

 So I say to you, ask, and it will be given to you; seek, and you will find; knock, and it will be opened to you (Luke 11:5-9).

Jesus says that it is your persistence that gets those prayers answered. In this passage, Jesus illustrates that the one who would not accept "no" for an answer got what he expected.

 Too many Christians accept just enough in life. It is time we expect and receive more.

Let me show you what my mom did to raise her expectations in life. At age 24 she could not read or drive. She had been told her whole life how dumb she was, how worthless she was. She could not be in a group of people, she was so shy. At age 24, she got saved, began to read the Bible, and found out that what she had been told was not true. She found out that she could have more. She then did what I will show you in just a moment.

The question is, how do we increase our hope? First, let's go to the Word and find out:

...that at that time you were without Christ, being aliens from the commonwealth of Israel and strangers from the covenants of promise, having no hope and without God in the world (Ephesians 2:12).

When we don't know the covenants and promises of God, we lack hope. Hope comes from knowing what God says we can have.

Now go to Romans 15:4:

For whatever things were written before were written for our learning, that we through the patience and comfort of the Scriptures might have hope.

According to this Scripture, the Word of God increases our hope. It also brings us patience and comfort.

You may be broke, but get into the Word and find out what His promises are regarding finances. Those promises will not only bring you hope, but patience and comfort as well. In other words, you are OK waiting for the substance of your hope to take material form.

Psalms 119:81 says,

My soul faints for Your salvation, but I hope in Your word.

Verse 114 continues that theme:

You are my hiding place and my shield; I hope in Your word.

Whose word do you hope in? Is it Constant Negative News (CNN)? Whose report do you believe? Do you believe what the world says about the economy? about marriage? about your life? Or do you put your hope in God's Word?

I know the world says there is no happiness in marriage. But God's Word says your wife is the greatest gift ever given to you. She is worth more than rubies. The word you believe determines what you get.

I am amazed at the number of Christians who watch the news. The average Christian watches two hours a day, filling his or her mind with all the negativity in the world. They turn it on first thing in the morning to set the mood for the whole day, and then watch it before bed so their mind can meditate on that all night long. They then wonder why they are down, depressed, and filled with low expections. Faith truly comes by hearing, and hearing by the word [of God]. (See Romans 10:17.)

If the word you are hearing is from the news, then that is where your hope will be. If you are hearing God's Word, your hope goes to another level.

Do you know how much news I listen to in a week? None! No news, no newspaper. "Well, Scot, how do you know what is going on in the world?" Well, to find out my future, I look at the Word. That tells me what to expect.

 I challenge you: for the next 30 days, neither watch nor listen to the news. Spend that time in the Word, building your hope.

You will see a dramatic change in what you expect out of life. This, of course, will change what you get out of life.

As you have seen, only one thing increases your hope. It is the word of God. "Faith comes by hearing and hearing by the word of God" (see Rom. 10:17).

A major consensus among psychologists today is that the only known method to change expectation is through hearing something over and over again. Those of a Judeo-Christian persuasion have known this for thousands of years.

This tells us that the Word isn't just a bunch of stories. One of its main purposes is to change and increase our expectations.

I challenge you to get into the Word. Don't just pick it up and start reading wherever. Write down areas in your life that don't feel right or aren't going right. Now look to the Word for a new expectation. Write those Scriptures down and meditate on them. Put them on your mirror, in your car, in your refrigerator. Keep that new expectation in front of you until you get it.

You may ask, "Pastor, how do I know when I've got it?" Easy, when that area in your life changes.

This is exactly what my mom did. At age 24, she began to write out Scriptures in a notebook and then confess them throughout the day. She actually made a necklace out of it and took it everywhere she went. While driving, momma was confessing the word (while Jason and I prayed in the backseat). She confessed that she had the mind of Christ, that she was blessed wherever she went, that she had favor, that she had the ability to obtain wealth. Momma made a three-minute tape of her voice quoting these Scriptures, and she played it 24 hours a day. Even today, every year she makes a new tape that plays 24 hours a day, 365 days a year.

Look at her life today. She is a multi-millionaire, who not only can read but is a best-selling author all over the world. Not only can she talk to people, but she is on TV every day, preaching the Gospel to an international audience.

You ask what took you from having nothing, being a nothing, to who you are in Christ today. She will immediately say *the Word of God*!

Action Steps

√   List areas in your life that you feel could get better.

√   Now write out your current expectations.

√   Go to the Word and research what the Word says about those areas in your life.

√   Now write out what your expectations need to be.

√   I challenge you to quote these Scriptures throughout the day. Take them wherever you go. If you want to take it to the next level, make a tape of your voice and play it 24 hours a day.

Key points and personal adaption

_____

_____

_____

_____

_____

_____

_____

_____

_____

_____

_____

_____

_____

_____

_____

_____

_____

_____

Chapter 7

Shooting Holes in the Poverty-Minded Christian's Religion!

For the most part, poverty-minded Christians have built their entire religion on a couple of Scriptures, even though there are far more Scriptures that talk about wealth than poverty. The poverty-minded, for whatever reason, hold onto these two biblical passages: First Timothy 6 and James 5. These are the two passages from which we get the "It is spiritual to be poor" mentality. I want to take a moment and explain these passages as they were intended to be interpreted.

James 5

Come now, you rich, weep and howl for your miseries that are coming upon you! Your riches are corrupted, and your garments are moth-eaten. Your gold and silver are corroded, and their corrosion will be a witness against you and will eat your flesh like fire. You have heaped up treasure in the last days. Indeed the wages of the laborers who mowed your fields, which you kept back by fraud, cry out; and the cries of the reapers have reached the ears of the Lord of Sabaoth. You have lived on the earth in pleasure and luxury; you have fattened your hearts as in a day of slaughter. You have condemned, you have murdered the just; he does not resist you (James 5:1-6).

This Scripture in no way is against you becoming wealthy. James is not condemning the possession of wealth. He is clearly warning those who get their wealth unjustly and live lavishly while ignoring their neighbors (see James 5:4-6). Wealthy people of that kind are storing up judgment for themselves (see James 5:1). God will call us to account for how we earn and spend our money.

Yes, if you lack character and rip people off to obtain your riches, then "what you sow, you shall reap" (see Gal. 6:7). If your money possesses you rather than being your possession, if you don't give, if you are not a blessing, then according to this passage, you have a harvest in your future that you probably won't want.

But if you earn your money using godly principles, living a life of character and integrity, then there is nothing wrong with obtaining the wealth God says He wants you to have. If your heart is to be a blessing and to further the Kingdom, then life is good. God says in Second Corinthians 9 that He wants you to have an abundance so you can give for every good work.

Most Christians can't give out of their abundance because they don't have it. They have to give a little out of their lack. In a lot of ways, I see poor Christians fulfilling more of that Scripture than the wealthy Christians I know. They aren't able to help their neighbors, because they can barely help themselves. All of their money goes to just getting by. I think that those who choose to be poor for religion's sake are very selfish. Every penny they make is just for them. But as for me, I give more per year than many give in a lifetime. Which way of thinking is more like God's heart?

I get so mad that pastors read the first part of this passage and preach entire sermons on why we shouldn't have money. Come on, people, let's read the whole Bible. Let's not just take someone's word for it. As I said earlier, this teaching produces no fruit. It holds back the Body of Christ.

Imagine this with me. Let's say in America, 100,000 people go to church in each state. The actual number is more than ten times that, according to a Gallup poll, but for the sake of argument, let's use this very conservative number. That means 5 million people attend church. Let's say each person becomes a millionaire. That is $5,000,000,000,000 ($5 trillion) that the Body of Christ controls.

OK, Church, we need 10 percent, which comes to $500,000,000,000—that is $500 billion! We could pay off every church building. We could put a Bible in every person's hand in the world. No one would have to go hungry. Everyone could have shelter. We could own all the television networks and put good programs on. We could buy all the movie studios and make movies of character and integrity. Wow, we just changed a world, and it took only 10 percent.

Imagine what would happen if we took out of our abundance and gave another 10 percent–or even 25 percent. Why does this make such good sense? Because it is right.

1 Timothy 6

If anyone teaches otherwise and does not consent to wholesome words, even the words of our Lord Jesus Christ, and to the doctrine which accords with godliness, he is proud, knowing nothing, but is obsessed with disputes and arguments over words, from which come envy, strife, reviling, evil suspicions, useless wranglings of men of corrupt minds and destitute of the truth, who suppose that godliness is a means of gain. From such withdraw yourself.

Now godliness with contentment is great gain. For we brought nothing into this world, and it is certain we can carry nothing out. And having food and clothing, with these we shall be content. But those who desire to be rich fall into temptation and a snare, and into many foolish and harmful lusts which drown men in destruction and perdition. For the love of money is a root of all kinds of evil, for which some have strayed from the faith in their greediness, and pierced themselves through with many sorrows (1 Timothy 6:3-10).

Let's break this passage down:

If anyone teaches otherwise and does not consent to wholesome words, even the words of our Lord Jesus Christ, and to the doctrine which accords with godliness, he is proud, knowing nothing, but is obsessed with disputes and arguments over words, from which come envy, strife, reviling, evil suspicions, useless wranglings of men of corrupt minds and destitute of the truth, who suppose that godliness is a means of gain. From such withdraw yourself.

Let me say first that this passage is not for the entire Body of Christ. Paul is speaking to leaders. Nevertheless, that doesn't especially matter here; I think this passage can apply to all our lives.

This passage is talking about those who teach contrary to the Word. They want to argue about everything. They want to argue about why I shouldn't have any money. Understand, I don't want to argue. I really don't care if they stay poor; furthermore, I have no argument. I just want people to know you don't have to be poor. That is not God's plan.

Paul is talking here about people arguing against the Word of God. He then talks about men with corrupt minds who suppose that godliness is a means of gain. Now, gain doesn't have to mean financial prosperity, though it may include it. Rather, this Scripture is talking about those pastors who preach, "Hey, give me $238 [based on the passage from Luke 2:38], and now God will give you a supernatural money miracle. Give me money, and God will give you money." Those gimmicks, of course, rarely work. I have seen people give and give and give—and never get. It is because God is concerned with the heart.

Malachi tells us God's plan, and the important part of it is the motive behind the gift.

"Bring all the tithes into the storehouse,
That there may be food in My house,
And try Me now in this,"

Says the Lord of hosts,
"If I will not open for you the windows of heaven
And pour out for you such blessing
That there will not be room enough to receive it.

"And I will rebuke the devourer for your sakes,
So that he will not destroy the fruit of your
ground,
Nor shall the vine fail to bear fruit for you in the
field,"
Says the Lord of hosts;
"And all nations will call you blessed,
For you will be a delightful land,"
Says the Lord of hosts (Malachi 3:10-12).

Why do we bring the tithes into the storehouse? What needs to be the motive of our hearts? God's answer is, "So there is food in My storehouse."

That has to be our heart and our attitude. If that is our motive, now the promises come our way. God will now open up the windows of Heaven and pour out a blessing we cannot contain. He will now rebuke the devourer on our behalf.

So Jesus answered and said, "Assuredly, I say to you,
there is no one who has left house or brothers or
sisters or father or mother or wife or children or
lands, for My sake and the gospel's, who shall not

receive a hundredfold now in this time... (Mark 10:29-30).

 If you give, your motive needs to be for Jesus' sake and the Gospel's sake.

If you do that, you are entitled to one hundredfold. God is all about the heart.

You ask someone, "Why did you give?"

"Well, the pastor gave this message and said I would get a hundredfold."

Well, the windows-of-Heaven blessing does not apply to you. You need to give so there is food in the storehouse.

"Well, Pastor, I gave because my wife was after me to give."

OK, that is great, but the hundredfold does not apply to your gift. That is for those who give for the Gospel's sake.

This is why you see people give and give and give, and nothing in their finances changes. The attitude of the heart is wrong.

Now, there is this fine line. I give for the Gospel's sake, but I do expect the blessings. I don't give because of the blessings, yet I do expect to be blessed. Let me give you an example.

When I get old, I expect my kids to take care of me. But today, I give to them because I love them. I want the best for them. I don't give to get, but I do expect to be taken care of.

I give to God because I love Him. I see Him as my source. All that I have is because of Him. He doesn't need my money; He needs my heart. Where my treasure is, there is my heart. I love to give. I give to further the Gospel; I give to help the Church and all of God's works. That is my heart. In that, I know God has no problem giving back to me.

I think this attitude keeps us in check when the money does come. God doesn't want to pour out the finances on those who don't see God as their source, on those who say, "I will give when I have money." That is a wrong attitude. The tithe is God's. It is saying, "God, You are my source." Guess what? If you are faithful in the little, you will be ruler over much. But if God can't trust you to give $100, why would He think you would ever give $100,000?

That passage in Timothy doesn't have to be about money. I think it has to do with life. I live a life full of biblical character, not because I will get, but because I love God. I do right because of the love of God, not because of what I will get. But in doing right, I can expect to have the life God wants me to have.

I don't do nice things for my wife because of what I will get. I love her because she exists. In that, I get a great marriage.

Let's continue with First Timothy 6:

Now godliness with contentment is great gain. For we brought nothing into this world, and it is certain we can carry nothing out. And having food and clothing, with these we shall be content.

I absolutely love this part. I strongly believe that we need to learn to be happy where we are and excited about where we are going.

Most people have formed the worldly belief, "I will be happy when I have…a big house…a new car…the biggest television ever."

I'm not saying there is anything wrong with having these things. I am saying that things cannot be the source of your happiness. If they are, you will never be happy, at least not for long.

The Bible says, "Rejoice in the Lord always. Again I will say, rejoice!" (Phil. 4:4). Paul's simple admonition to rejoice is not based on anything external—not on circumstances or on possessions.

I was happy living in a 900-square foot apartment, sharing an old Honda with my wife. I am happy today having a lot more. I have always been happy, no matter what I have. We need to live by this.

"But, Pastor, you don't understand my circumstances."

Well, Paul was in prison when he said, "Rejoice!" Come on, people, learn to be happy with just some food and clothes. Be happy where you are at and excited about where God is taking you.

> *But those who desire to be rich* [a closer translation says if being rich is all they are after, if money is their strongest desire] *fall into temptation and a snare, and into many foolish and harmful lusts which drown men in destruction and perdition. For the love of money is a root of all kinds of evil, for which some have strayed from the faith in their greediness, and pierced themselves through with many sorrows* (1 Timothy 6:9-10).

The Message Bible says it like this:

> *But if it's only money these leaders are after, they'll self-destruct in no time. Lust for money brings trouble and nothing but trouble. Going down that path, some lose their footing in the faith completely and live to regret it bitterly ever after.*

Yes, when money becomes what life is all about, life will not be good. You gain the whole world, but you lose your soul. You have lots of money, but your kids want nothing to do with you. You've got the big house and boat, but you've lost another marriage.

Once again, relationships have to be most important. They are what life is all about. It is about others and loving them. As I said earlier, when money becomes more valuable to you than people, you are headed toward destruction. But as long as we keep our values in check, life is good.

Paul says don't allow greed to take you from your faith. Don't allow money to become more important than people, more important than your relationship with God. If you build your finances on the Word of God, life can be awesome.

I'm sure some other Scriptures may be pulled out of context to try to keep Christians broke and miserable, but these are the most commonly used. They all come down to the same thing: if you are God and want your representatives (we Christians) to change the world, keeping them broke makes no sense because bringing change costs money. Once again, imagine what you could do for the Body of Christ if you were a multimillionaire.

Action Steps

√   Choose three of the heroes of the faith in the Bible, such as Abraham, Moses, Joshua, or David, and read about their lives. Were they poor people who depended on others to get by? Or were they blessed people who could bless others?

√   Consider your heart's motive for giving. Has it been to bless or to receive in return for your giving? What can you do to be a cheerful giver?

√   Decide how you would use $100,000 to further the Gospel if you had it right now to give. Now decide how you would give $100.

√   Write down your top priorities. Are you spending your time and your money in line with those priorities? How can you make adjustments?

√   Imagine what you could do for the Body of Christ if you were a multimillionaire.

Key points and personal adaption

Chapter 8

God Is a Good God—All the Time

My youngest son, Peyton, was given 4,000 lady-bugs by his Aunt Kimmy. He had a bag of bugs, and he just loved watching them. He would put his hand in the bag and feel them on his skin. He had one in particular that he singled out. It was his little buddy. He called it RoRo, after a dog we used to have named Romeo. Peyton loved to take RoRo around and play with his little friend. I watched them having fun. Peyton said, "Come on, RoRo," and they went all over the place.

But then, after a while, Peyton's tone changed. The ladybug stopped cooperating. Peyton shouted, "Come here!" But the ladybug didn't move. "RoRo, now!"

He kept ordering RoRo to come, and when RoRo didn't come, he got mad and in a moment of passion, stomped on him. RoRo was no more.

Too many Christians seem to think that God treats us the same way. If they get a little bit out of line, He will stomp on them. They believe that He sends them sickness or He keeps them poor so that they can learn lessons and be humble.

In the spirit of making Christianity look appealing, let's get rid of the religious fallacy that God is out to get us, that He beats us up, that He takes away our money, and that He gives us cancer to teach us a lesson. If you read in the paper that I had given my kids cancer to teach them a lesson, what kind of father would you say I was? I would be one of the worst fathers ever.

How in the world can anyone in a right mind say something like that about God, or even worse, believe it?

I don't know about your daddy, but my Daddy is a good one. My God wants me blessed. He wants me happy. He wants me to have a great, amazing life. That is a good father.

 If a son asks for bread from any father among you, will he give him a stone? Or if he asks for a fish, will he give him a serpent instead of a fish? Or if he asks for an egg, will he offer him a scorpion? If you then, being evil, know how to give good gifts to your children, how much more will your heavenly Father give the Holy Spirit to those who ask Him... (Luke 11:11-13).

Yes, I need to follow His Word to have a great life. Yes, when I step outside His will, bad things tend to happen. But the point is that He doesn't send the bad stuff. He knows the bad stuff is out there. That is why He says, "Follow My Word." If you speed down the highway, God does not send a cop to give you a ticket. The ticket is just a thing that happens when you break the law. If you eat wrong, don't exercise, and you get sick, God did not send the sickness. Sickness is the result of not eating right.

 If, deep down inside, you believe God is not good, both your relationship with Him and your experience in life will be greatly hindered.

If any of my sons thought I sent them sickness or harm, I guarantee that they would have trouble getting close to me and allowing me to have a close relationship with them.

 For let not that man suppose that he will receive anything from the Lord; he is a double-minded man, unstable in all his ways (James 1:7-8).

You have to be convinced that God is a good God all of the time. If you think that God is beating you up all the time, letting all of those bad things happen to you, then you will quickly lose your motivation to try. How can you fight God? If He's against you, then you may as well just sit down and suffer in silence.

When my children think that something bad is happening, they get very de-motivated to do anything. When they believe that I am good and that I want the best for them, they are motivated to conquer everything they face. It is an attitude in life that flows from their relationship with me.

The same is true with how you view God. When you realize that He does not do bad things to you, it changes your whole outlook on life. Instead of being angry with God about a problem you run into, you partner with Him to solve it.

The truth is that God wants you to prosper and be healthy. The lessons He wants you to learn are the ones that you get from participating with Him in solving the problems of life and overcoming every obstacle you run into.

 Get it through your head right now that God is good. Otherwise your life will be a long, hard road.

Action Steps

√   Consider how you feel about God deep down. Do you believe He is for you? If not, begin confronting your thoughts and feelings with what the Word of God says about His love for you.

√   Are you facing any negative consequences resulting from your actions? How can you follow God's Word in the future to avoid these difficulties?

√   Talk to God about a problem you are facing. Allow Him to help you solve it.

Key points and personal adaption

_____

_____

_____

_____

_____

_____

_____

_____

_____

_____

_____

_____

_____

Chapter 9

As the World Would Say, "#$%@ Happens!"

Why, then, do bad things happen? Even more importantly, why do bad things happen to good people?

I have a teaching on why bad things happen. Using the story of Joseph, I go through his life. Few could argue they have had a harder life than Joseph. I show that there are three reasons why bad things happen. But if we allow it, God can make all things good.

 We know that all things work together for good to those who love God, to those who are called according to His purpose (Romans 8:28).

Why Bad Things Happen

Reason Number One: We make bad choices. The simple truth is, most of the bad things that have happened in your life came from your bad choices. You chose not to be a great spouse. You chose the job you are in, the life you are living. You made a lot of choices, and each of them produced something in your life. Joseph chose to tell his brothers and father about his dream. It's pretty stupid to tell your older brothers that they will worship you one day, especially when daddy already treats you like the favorite. It's probably not a good choice to wear the coat of many colors in front of them. Joseph's choices got him thrown into slavery.

Reason Number Two: Other people make choices. Yes, other people's choices affect you. You are living a good life, and someone backs into your car. Is it because God was teaching you a lesson? No! The other person just wasn't paying attention.

A number of years ago, a dad kidnapped his two-year-old child, and then burned her in the car. I had a guy ask me how I could believe in a God who allowed that to happen. (It's interesting how God gets blamed for anything bad that happens, but no credit is given to Him for any good.)

My answer is simple. That is a consequence of free will. God gave us free will and the ability to choose. With that comes good and bad. In a lot of ways, I'm glad God can't make me do something. I'm glad that if some ugly woman with a beard prays I will leave my wife and fall in love with her, God does not honor her prayer. I have a free will; I can make my own choices. And God will never go against our free will.

What is interesting is that the school teacher in this case said she didn't feel right about letting the two-year-old go with her father. That was God saying, "Don't do it," but that stupid free will decided otherwise. The guy got pulled over by a cop. The cop said he thought something wasn't right. Once again, God was trying, but the free will of the cop didn't heed the warning. It is very sad, but people's free will and their choices affect us. The little girl's story is very sad. Was it God's fault? Of course not. Was it God's will? Of course not. It was God's plan for her to live a long, healthy life, but bad choices took that away.

Your husband decides to run off with someone else. Sure, there are things you could have done differently as a wife, but more than likely it was in him. It was just a matter of time, or a matter of opportunity, before it happened. Now you are stuck with two kids by yourself. It is not fair; it is just a bad thing.

Go back to Joseph. He was an amazing employee, the best in the house. Potiphar's wife chose to go after him. He did the right thing and said, "No." And he went to jail. It's not fair, not right. Yet Joseph still gave his all, even in jail.

The same applies to many of you. Don't give up. Yes, raising kids alone is hard, but if you do all you can—grow, and change, and get financially literate—you will step right out of that into God's blessings.

 If you become a victim of your problems, your problems will never change.

Finally, Reason Number Three: Bad stuff happens just because. I don't know how else to say it. The world says, "#$%@ happens!" Yes, it does. For Joseph, it was a famine. It happened. For me, a tithing, Bible-believing guy who lives a great life, it was waking up one day with a foot of water in the basement. Was it God teaching me a lesson? Of course not. It just happened. Did it ruin my day? Of course not. Every day is a great day. God turned it around, and I got all new flooring from the insurance payment. Thank You, God, for turning it around for good. For Joseph, bad things helped raise him up to second in command in his nation. Yes, things happen in life. Do all you can, and God will take you to the next level.

Action Steps

√   Memorize Romans 8:28 and repeat it daily.

√   Review your current situation. What choices did you make in the past that have resulted in positive outcomes? What poor choices have you made? Ask God for wisdom to make good choices going forward.

√   Make a plan to become more financially literate.

√   Think of two or three situations where something bad happened and God turned it around to bless you. Thank Him for that.

√   Refuse to be a victim. Give your best no matter what you are facing and don't give up!

Key points and personal adaption

_____

_____

_____

_____

_____

_____

_____

_____

_____

_____

_____

_____

_____

_____

_____

Chapter 10

Jesus Wasn't Poor

The popular conception of Jesus for nearly all of the past 2,000 years has been that of a poor, very spiritual, wise Man, traveling through the towns of Israel, doing miracles, and teaching while He lived in abject poverty as an example of God's perfect will. The fact that this image is the opposite of what the Bible actually shows doesn't even seem to register with many Christians. The mindset is so strong that they don't see the truth even when they read it.

My purpose in this chapter is to dispel that image of Jesus and to show that He was, in fact, anything but poor. The material here is a summary of a chapter from my dad's book, *Becoming a Millionaire God's Way* (by C. Thomas Anderson). I strongly suggest that you get this book. It is probably one of the finest books written on finances.

It is important to have an accurate picture of Jesus' life. If you believe Jesus was poor, and that we should be like Jesus, then you will develop a poverty mindset. It will continue to keep you from wealth. If you really believe that Jesus was poor, then every time you get ahead financially, you will start to feel guilty about it, and you will unconsciously find ways to lose it. (After all, you don't want to be a second-class Christian, and you are convinced that money makes you exactly that.)

This belief about Jesus has been around almost as long as the Church. It began officially in the third century. The New Testament Church did not preach poverty at all. That was something that started over a hundred years later.

It came from early Greek philosophy. Nearly every Greek school of thought taught that the material world was flawed and that only the spiritual could be perfect. Consequently, anything physical, including money, had to be of lesser value than spiritual things. This led to the idea that in order to be spiritual, you had to be separated from anything of the physical world—from all pleasure, and from all money.

As the Church started to spread through the Gentile world, many of the pagan beliefs and philosophies started to slip into the Church's life. People with a pagan background got saved, and they brought many of their old thought patterns in with them. It wasn't long before the Church began to think of righteousness in the same terms as the pagans—suffering and poverty. At first, this was easy because the Christians were so often persecuted. They really did suffer for their faith, and many were martyred, especially under the Roman emperors Domitian and Nero. These martyrs were praised as the heroes of the faith, and it became popular to associate with them and their suffering. When Christianity became recognized under Emperor Constantine, the blatant persecution stopped.

The belief that suffering was good, however, continued on as a religious tradition. Most of the Church believed that if they weren't suffering, they weren't spiritual. Since no one was persecuting them anymore, they began to look for ways that they could inflict suffering on themselves. The pagan ideal of giving up material possessions quickly became a part of this misguided notion of righteousness.

Instead of using the time of freedom to spread the Gospel throughout the world, many people began to isolate themselves from the world, living in monasteries and in caves. The ideals of poverty and suffering, neither of which can be found in biblical sources, mixed together to almost completely stop the fulfillment of the Great Commission to preach the Gospel to the whole world.

One of the verses in the Bible most frequently used to support this belief was Matthew 19:21:

If you want to be perfect, go, sell what you have and give to the poor, and you will have treasure in heaven....

Jesus made this statement to a rich young man who was so attached to his money that it completely controlled his life.

 Jesus didn't say that people should be poor; He just said that people shouldn't allow their money to control them.

It was another way of saying that you are to be blessed to be a blessing, not blessed so you can be selfish. God wants you to be rich because it takes money to fulfill the Great Commission to go into all the world and preach the Gospel. That's really hard to do when you don't even have enough money to go out of your house. You just can't go into all the world if you're broke.

Jesus was never controlled by money, but He always had plenty of it to support His ministry. He knew the right way to use it. The belief that Jesus was poor did not come from the Bible; it has produced very destructive fallacies in people's minds. Here are a few things that you should think about.

Jesus Became Poor to Make Us Rich

The Bible only mentions one time that Jesus was poor. That was on the cross.

For you know the grace of our Lord Jesus Christ, that though He was rich, yet for your sakes He became poor, that you through His poverty might become rich (2 Corinthians 8:9).

And Paul wasn't just talking about spiritual things. In the next chapter, verse 11, he specifically says "enriched in everything," or, as the NIV puts it, "You will be made rich in every way" (2 Cor. 9:11). "Every way" includes both spiritual and material riches. It means every way that you can be rich—and money is certainly one of them. The reason Jesus became poor was so that we could become rich. According to Second Corinthians 5:21, Jesus took all of our sins on Himself so that we could be free of them. He became sin so that we could have righteousness. He became sorrow so we could have joy. He became poor so that we could be rich.

He was only poor during those three hours on the cross. During His ministry leading up to the cross, He was rich. After He rose from the grave, He became rich again. Jesus never stayed poor.

Jesus was the Word of God according to the first chapter of John, and the Word never had to do without.

He always had everything He needed. He was the Creator of the entire universe (see John 1:1). He could call on unlimited resources.

God…has in these last days spoken to us by His Son, whom He has appointed heir of all things, through whom also He made the worlds; who being the brightness of His glory and the express image of His person, and upholding all things by the word of His power… (Hebrews 1:1-3).

 The plain truth is that if you think of Jesus as poor, then you see God as poor.

If God is poor, then He is also weak and powerless. But God can't be weak. And since Jesus is God, neither can He.

We are joint heirs with Jesus, meaning that everything that is His is also ours.

But God…even when we were dead in trespasses, made us alive together with Christ (by grace you have been saved), and raised us up together, and made us sit together in the heavenly places in Christ Jesus (Ephesians 2:4-6).

That means that if Jesus isn't poor, we aren't poor either.

The Life of Jesus

Most Christians have gotten so used to being told that Jesus was poor that they read the Gospels and don't even notice how many times the Bible indicates that Jesus was rich. We won't find a verse that comes right out and says, "Jesus wasn't poor," but we don't have to look very far to see the obvious indications that He had plenty of money. Here are a few things you may not have noticed.

1. Jesus was born in the royal line of David.

The genealogies of Jesus, which are given in Matthew 1:1-17 and Luke 3:23-38, show that Jesus had royal blood. On both Mary's side of the family and Joseph's, He could follow His lineage back to King David. In addition, on Mary's side, He was connected to the priesthood. Both of these things brought a higher status in the society of ancient Israel. Jesus had to learn early in life how to move in high society. He was among the wealthy, the leaders, from the earliest age. He rubbed shoulders with the wealthy and the influential. He went to prestigious banquets given by important people.

2. The inn was full.

Many people seem to think that Mary and Joseph stayed in a cave or barn the night Jesus was born because they couldn't afford to stay at the inn. They sing traditional Christmas songs with lyrics like, "Away in a manger, no crib for a bed, the little Lord Jesus lays down His sweet head." The Bible never says that. It says that the inn was full. There was no vacancy (see Luke 2:7).

3. The manger was the best place to be.

It probably worked out for the best that they couldn't find a place in the inn. The cave was undoubtedly warmer and more comfortable. Inns in those days were not like modern motels. They were a simple enclosure with rooms that faced in. They had no furniture or comforts of any kind. You put your animals inside so that they wouldn't wander off during the night and so no predators could get at them. Then you picked a room and threw a blanket on the floor.

The cave where Jesus was put in the manger was nearby the inn. It was much better protection from the cold than the inn would have been. As it turned out, Jesus was better off there. Mary and Joseph were probably thanking God that He had provided so well for them.

4. Mary and Joseph had a house in Bethlehem.

It wasn't all that long before Mary and Joseph moved out of the cave and into a house. Matthew makes it clear that they lived in a house by the time the wise men arrived.

And when they had come into the house, they saw the young Child with Mary His mother, and fell down and worshiped Him... (Matthew 2:11).

Money obviously wasn't the issue. They had plenty of money to get a good place to stay. They just had to wait a short time before the house they wanted was available.

5. The Magi brought expensive gifts.

Mary and Joseph don't appear to have been poor before Jesus was born, but even if they were, it didn't last very long. When the wise men came, they brought some of the most expensive stuff available in the ancient world.

...And when they had opened their treasures, they presented gifts to Him: gold, frankincense, and myrrh (Matthew 2:11).

We know from the account in Matthew 2 that the wise men did not come the same night as the birth of Jesus. It may have been closer to two years later. We know that because Herod asked the wise men when the star had appeared. Later, using that information, he had every child in Bethlehem under the age of two killed (see Matt. 2:16). That may mean that the wise men had been on the road for nearly two years, leaving when the star appeared at Jesus' birth and arriving a couple of years later.

It doesn't take much thought to figure out that diplomats from a foreign nation will not travel more than a year to bring a card and a box of candy. They came with gifts that were fit for a king. They brought gold. One of the gifts was frankincense, a very valuable kind of incense. They also had myrrh, which at that time was considered more valuable than gold. The gifts were worth a lot of money. And to go to all that trouble, you can bet they didn't bring just a little. There had to be a substantial amount of each.

6. Jesus was well-educated.

When Jesus was 12 years old, His parents took Him to the Temple. On the way home, they discovered that He was missing, and it took them three days to find Him (see Luke 2:41-50).

He was in the Temple courtyard all that time, discussing matters of theology with the most educated men in the country. If Jesus was just a poor peasant child, they would not have let Him sit in on those discussions. As it was, they not only let Him listen, but they were amazed at how much He knew and understood. He was well-educated, which means that His parents must have been well enough off to afford a good education.

7. The first miracle was a miracle of luxury, performed in a setting of wealth.

The first miracle that Jesus performed was turning water into wine at a wedding in Cana (see John 2:1-11). We can learn a couple of important things from this.

First of all, Jesus got invited to high society events. This was obviously a big wedding, and Cana was a very wealthy area in Jesus' day. The fact that running out of wine was such an embarrassment to the host indicates that it had to be a wealthy wedding. If it were a poor family, that wouldn't have mattered. Also, it was a wedding to which the wealthy would have been invited. This implies that Jesus and His family were wealthy enough to be included.

Another interesting thing is that the miracle was really not necessary. No one was healed or delivered. No one got raised from the dead. No one's life depended on it. Jesus did a miracle that was primarily designed to let people keep on drinking. It was a miracle of extravagance. It was all about luxury. Jesus obviously didn't have a problem with wealth or with the extra comforts that wealth brought.

8. The disciples were successful businessmen.

When Jesus chose the 12 apostles, He didn't call men who were out of work. He chose men who were successful businessmen and professionals. Peter, Andrew, John, and James all had fishing businesses (see Matt. 4:18-22). Matthew was a tax collector (see Matt. 9:9). Tax collectors were well known for being wealthy.

These were not losers standing in the unemployment line. Jesus looked for men who had proven that they knew how to work and they knew how to be successful and productive.

If Jesus was really poor, successful men would never have followed Him. They would have considered Him to be a failure in life.

The rich follow the rich.

The poor follow the rich.

But the rich don't follow the poor.

9. The disciples didn't question Jesus' ability to spend a fortune.

When Jesus fed the 5,000, it is interesting to see how He set His disciples up for the miracle. They wanted Him to send the crowd away, since it was late in the day and everyone was hungry. Jesus told them to feed the crowd themselves (see Mark 6:37).

They replied that it would take two hundred *denarii* to feed that many people. The amount given in John 6:7 was about eight months' wages.

Of course, we know that Jesus took a little bread and some fish and miraculously multiplied it, but what we don't usually see is that the disciples never questioned Jesus' finances. They assumed that there was enough money on hand to buy that much food. In Mark, they said it this way: "Shall we go and buy two hundred denarii worth of bread and give them something to eat?" (Mark 6:37). If Jesus didn't have that much money, their question wouldn't have made sense. He had plenty of money. That wasn't the issue.

10. Jesus needed a treasurer to keep track of the money.

As we just saw, Jesus had plenty of money for whatever situation came up. In fact He had so much that He needed a treasurer to take care of it. John 13:29 tells us that Judas was appointed for that task. When Jesus needed something purchased, He sent Judas to do it.

The reason they needed so much money was because Jesus traveled with a large group of people. It wasn't just the 12. The number grew to at least 70 at some point (see Luke 10:1). A group of women also followed Him (see Luke 8:1-3; 23:49). It took quite a bit of money just to feed them all. Jesus ran a large budget operation.

11. Jesus could pour a year's wages on the ground and not miss it.

One day, Jesus was staying at a place in the town of Bethany, when a woman came in and poured a flask of very expensive perfume on Him, as a way of worshiping Him (see Matt. 26:7). The perfume was worth a year's wages—what would be about $40,000 dollars today.

The disciples were shocked. They thought it was a terrible waste. At the very least, they thought that the perfume should have been sold and the money given to the poor. (They did seem to understand the idea of being blessed to be a blessing.)

Jesus didn't have a problem with such extravagant waste, however. He thought it was a noble gesture.

> *"Why do you trouble the woman? For she has done a good work for Me. For you have the poor with you always, but Me you do not have always. For in pouring this fragrant oil on My body, she did it for My burial."* (Matthew 26:10-12).

Apparently, Jesus saw something more to life than just giving everything away to the poor. Jesus understood a basic principle. No matter how much you give to the poor, you will still have the poor with you because they will continue to be poor. Some are poor in the first place, but then they choose to remain poor, rather than believing the word of prosperity.

Jesus had no problem with pouring $40,000 out onto someone's head. He wasn't bound by the kind of belief system that turns away from material possessions and the extravagant use of them.

Biblical Prosperity

When you read the Gospels without a preconceived notion that it is spiritual to be broke and struggling, it becomes obvious that Jesus was not poor. He could preach to the wealthy and the poor because He was wealthy Himself. He could operate in the highest levels of society because He belonged there.

 Jesus called us to preach the Gospel the same way that He did. To do that, we must become like Him.

It is impossible to influence every level of society if we are not allowed into every level of society.

If you are poor, you can take the Gospel to the poor, but the rich will never listen to you. In fact, it's not likely that the poor will listen to you very often. You don't have anything to offer that they would be interested in. It is only when you are in a position to influence all of society that you can become most effective. You are blessed to be a blessing. If you do not believe in that blessing, then you will not be a blessing.

Action Steps

√   Reread one of the Gospels and write down all the evidence that Jesus was well off.

√   Consider your mindset about whether it's spiritual to be poor and struggling. How can you bring your thinking into line with the Word of God?

√   Make a list of what you are doing to fulfill the Great Commission. What else can you do?

√   Come up with one way you can position yourself in order to influence more people (join a networking group, take a class, etc.). Then act on it.

Key points and personal adaption

_____

_____

_____

_____

_____

_____

_____

_____

_____

_____

_____

_____

_____

_____

Chapter 11

Pastor vs. Pastor: God Wants You Poor vs. God Wants You Rich

Which is it? Does our Father in Heaven want us to just get by, or does our Daddy want us successful? Does our Heavenly Father want just some of His kids successful? Does He play favorites? These questions are all over the media, magazines, television. It seems that every time I turn on Larry King, it is one pastor and his belief that God wants us blessed vs. another pastor and his belief that money isn't for everyone. Here are two great pastors with two very different messages.

From listening to a particular debate, I have gathered that one pastor believes that God does not want everyone to be rich, while the other believes that God wants everyone to be richly blessed.

I think it is sad to hear a pastor who has no financial needs say money is not for everyone. Is he saying God wants money only for His favorites? I wonder if his teaching would change if he were raising five kids on welfare and struggling to pay the rent. "Oops, sorry. God doesn't want blessings for you."

I understand he is saying that money can't be the most important thing. I believe this is so true. Once again, relationships are. But what happens is that people take the excuse that money isn't everything, and they don't do anything financially for their lives.

They say, "Well, you don't need money to be happy." That is very true. I have been broke, and I was happy, and I am rich, and I am happy. (I will say, however, it is easier to be happy with money than it is without.) Money is not the source of happiness; relationships are. I understand that you don't need money to be happy, but money can make life a lot easier.

Some moms want to stay home with the kids, but money keeps them from living the desire of their hearts. If this is you, imagine that you have the finances to be a stay-at-home mom. For some of you ladies, that would allow you to do what you have dreamed of. Imagine if you could take the family on that three-week vacation and strengthen the relationship. Imagine what you could do for your church, for the missionaries, for all those around you. Imagine what you could do in life if you didn't have to worry about money.

Take away the excuse that God wants you to be poor, and begin to think some new thoughts: Now I need to get rich. I need to read books. I need to listen to audio messages. I am growing in the financial sense, changing my life from the inside out. I need to start a business, or buy some investments. My money is going to work for me instead of me working for my money.

 If you believe that money will destroy you, or that it is evil, then you will struggle your whole life through.

One of the pastors who believes that money isn't for everyone has published a great book on purpose. Yes, life is about purpose, but, as I said earlier, most people don't live a life of purpose because it takes all they have just to pay the bills. Let's break out of that and change our thinking. Let's take back the wealth. Let's get it into our hands. Now we can go forth and live a life full of purpose and destiny.

"Well, Pastor, everyone can't be rich."

Why not? Most of us have adopted the world's pie mentality. That is not how God operates. The pie mentality says if I want a bigger piece of the pie, you have to get a smaller piece. There is only so much pie. If I'm rich, how can you be rich? There is only so much money.

 God's Kingdom does not operate under the pie mentality. It is more like an endless river.

Take as much as you want, and there will still be plenty for everyone else.

Why can't all Christians be prosperous? Who will work the jobs? Let the world work the jobs. They can work for us. We have been working for them long enough. We have been lining their pockets long enough. It is time that their efforts go toward the building of His Kingdom.

I will say this about the pastor who wrote the book about purpose. In a sense, I feel that he did what my book talks about. He was blessed to be a blessing. He took from his abundance and paid back to the church every dime it gave to him. That is awesome: blessed to be a blessing.

Why shouldn't everyone be able to do that?

Action Steps

√   Plan some quality time to strengthen your family relationships. If you are single, plan some time with a good friend.

√   Imagine what you could do if money were no object. Which of these dreams do you believe are God's will for you? Ask Him to help you make them a reality.

√   Pick your next book to read (or audio message to listen to—I heard Scot's book on *21 days* is great) about finances after this one. If you don't have it, order it now.

√   Find someone whom you can bless now with something you have already been blessed with.

Key points and personal adaption

_____

_____

_____

_____

_____

_____

_____

_____

_____

_____

_____

_____

_____

_____

_____

_____

The following chapters are taken from two of my other books. Chapter 12 is a part of *Think Like a Billionaire, Become a Billionaire*. Chapters 13 through 15 are from *Millionaire Habits in 21 Days*. I include them here because they deal with how you think about money—which is really the whole problem that most Christians have with money. They don't think the way God wants them to think. Change your thinking, and you will change your world.

Chapter 12

One Change *Will* Produce Wealth

After interviewing numerous multi-millionaires, reading more than 20 books on becoming a millionaire, and listening to nearly 400 hours of CDs on getting wealthy, I have come to a conclusion, a conclusion that literally changed my life in just one year. This conclusion took me from having a net worth of maybe $250,000, that is, if I sold everything—the 401(k), the equity in the house, even the kids—to over $3 million in just one year. That's a net worth of more than 12 times where I started, with another $15 million worth of projects going. If I continue on that pace, I should be a billionaire in the next five to ten years.

What is interesting is that it took only one change, only one thing that I had to do differently. That one thing is what this message is all about. If you apply what you learn in this chapter, you will follow the same one-year journey. If you do this one thing, you, too, will be on your way to becoming a billionaire.

The one thing is so simple, yet I spent 37 years of my life avoiding it. It was so easy, yet it is the one thing we all avoid. I had to change the way I thought. Yes, that is it. When I changed the way I thought, I began to change what I did, which then changed the results in my life. It was so simple, yet it took 37 years for me to grab hold of it and actually do it.

Proverbs 23:7 says that as a man thinks, so is he. If I begin to think like a billionaire, biblically my life has no choice but to produce it. Where you are today is a collection of the thoughts you had yesterday; where you go tomorrow is based on your thoughts today. If you can think like the 5 percent who are the wealthy, in a matter of time, you will be part of the 5 percent. If you continue to think like the 95 percent, which represents the average person, you will remain average. You will live a life of just enough—save just enough to retire, maybe get a Winnebago, and live off your 401(k) or Social Security. But if you start thinking like a billionaire, you begin to step into the area God wants you to be in, the land of abundance.

Jesus said that out of the treasure of your heart, you will bring forth either good or evil (see Luke 6:45). Whatever is in your heart will be produced in the world. If what is average or mediocre is in your heart, then that is what will reproduce itself. If abundance is in your heart, then abundance will create itself in your world.

When I really boiled all the interviews, books, CDs, and get-rich-quick gimmicks down, I found out that the wealthy think differently than the rest of us. That is why you could take all of Donald Trump's money away, and in just a short amount of time, because of the way he thinks, he would be right back where he is today. How Trump thinks, so is he.

Billionaires think differently. They think differently about seven things in particular: Money, Investing, Jobs, Risks, Wisdom, and Time.

Money

Billionaires think differently about what money is for. We see money as a way to get things. They see money as a tool to invest. We need more money to get a bigger house, a nicer car, a bigger television. Billionaires see money as a tool to be used to make more money. Once they get an abundance, a portion of that is used for the finer things in life. Billionaires use a little for the extras of life, and a major portion to create an abundance for life. We use a major portion on the things of life, and a little bit to invest (into 401(k)s, or to dabble in the stock market) so we can get by in life.

As soon as we get some extra money, we look to where we can spend it. The rich immediately look to where they can invest it. We finally get that raise, and right away we go out and get a nicer car because we can now afford an extra $250 car payment. We can now go down and get that big screen television and make payments on it for the next five years. The wealthy, when they first start, say, "We'll drive what we are driving, watch what we are watching, and through investing, turn that $250 a month into millions. Then we can buy those things out of our abundance." We buy out of our lack. They buy out of their abundance.

 The rich see money as a tool. We see money as a way to buy stuff.

We buy today, pay a lot more tomorrow. They invest today, buy a lot more tomorrow.

Investing

We see investing as something we do just to have enough to retire. The wealthy see it as something you do to produce an abundance. We invest in 401(k)s and perhaps in stocks (off of a tip someone who knows nothing about stocks gave us). We know nothing about investing, so we tend not to do it very well.

The wealthy see investing as a priority. So they are constantly reading, studying, learning all they can about investing. The rest of us glance at the business section and read a report or two on Yahoo stock. They spend a significant portion of their lives learning how to be great investors. We spend a moment of time reading about how the wealthy made their money investing, all the while saying, "How come that never happens to me? That guy got so lucky!" No, he wasn't lucky; he was prepared. *Luck* always favors the prepared. He thought differently, and that different thinking made him lucky.

To us, investing isn't a priority. Because it is not a priority, we don't have much to invest with. Investing isn't even something we budget into our lives. We budget for clothes, going out, vacations, televisions, golf clubs, and all the stuff in life. The rich, when they started out, budgeted around their investments. We budget around our stuff.

We see investing as a means for retirement. The wealthy see it as a way to catapult them into abundance. For them, investing is the key to abundance. To us, investing is the key to having just enough when we retire.

Jobs

We think that if we could just get a better job, we would be rich. What is funny is that if Trump lost his money, I guarantee that finding a great job would not be his priority. Trump would be looking for an investment.

The rich believe that your money should work for you. We believe that we should work for our money.

"Oh, if I just had a better job. If I could just get that promotion, I would be rich."

No, you would make more money, but you would not be rich. I know people who make six-figure salaries who could sell everything they have, and their net worth would be under a few hundred thousand dollars. Yes, they have the big house, the big car, all the perks of life. Yet they are not wealthy. Many times I have seen a person who was making $200,000 a year lose not only the job, but everything. I have heard that nearly 75 percent of all NFL football players claim bankruptcy after they stop playing.

The wealthy see their jobs as a tool to get money to invest. We see our jobs as a tool to get money for stuff. Think about it. You probably make $20,000 to $30,000 more a year than you did ten years ago. Where is the money? What did you do with last year's $5,000 raise? New furniture? A boat? A car? Maybe you don't even know. Ten years ago, at the end of the month, after paying all the bills, you had $37 left over. Today, when you are making nearly twice as much, you have $37 left over. Unless you change your thinking, ten years from now, you will have $37 left over.

Unless we change our thinking, it will not matter how much money we make. We will never become wealthy.

If Trump lost all of his money, he would not go looking for a great job to make his millions. He might get a job, but the purpose of the job would be to give him money to invest. That should be the purpose of your job.

To the wealthy person, the job is there strictly to maintain your current living situation while giving you as much money to invest as possible—because it will be the investing that produces wealth, not the job.

We have to begin to see our money as seed to be sown. The Bible says that God gives seed to the sower (see 2 Cor. 9:10). That doesn't just mean the person who sows into the church. It also means the person who sows into investments. Consider the parable of the talents. What happened to the guy who just held onto his money? It was taken away and given to the one who invested.

Look around you. Who is the money being given to? The one who is sowing it, not the one who is hoarding it or spending it. Most of us, because we have the same attitude as the one who lost his money, say, "But I was afraid to invest. I was afraid I would lose it." Because of that thinking, we never get the abundance we should have.

When we think that our jobs are the way to economic freedom, we have taken God and put Him into a box. We take a limitless God and put limits on Him. There is one thing God cannot do, and that is go against the will of a person. I don't care how much you pray and fast, put on sackcloth, and run around, God cannot make your boss give you a raise. God cannot make your boss promote you. Your boss will not wake up one morning and go, "You know what? Scot isn't that good of an employee, but I think I will cut my own salary and give him a big raise." Do you see how God is limited?

But if you begin to invest, God says, "Now I have something to work with." You have now taken God out of the box and said, "God, You are limitless. Do Your thing."

God says, "I give seed to the sower." He says, "Scot was faithful with the little I gave him. I will make him ruler over much." The Bible says that God will bless whatever you put your hands to. The problem is that most of us are only putting our hands on our remote control. And yes, we do have the best television around. But when you start to put your hands into investments, God begins to pour out into all your endeavors.

Risks

We don't take risks because we are afraid we will fail. What if it doesn't work? The rich think that if they don't take risks, they have already failed.

We ask, "What if the business goes belly up? I will be a failure." The rich think, "If I don't take a chance on the business, I am a failure."

We live in a world that has God unemployed. We make all our bill payments, our VISA and MasterCard payments, and car payments. We can do all that on our own. We really don't need God.

God so desperately wants us in a place where we need Him, where we step out and say, "OK, God, for me, this is impossible. But with You, nothing is impossible." In this way, I have employed God. I have given Him something to do in my life. We are now working together. The Bible says that God directs our steps. It doesn't say He directs our sitting. We don't just sit back and wait for God to drop a million-dollar idea in our laps. We start to step out. Once we take some steps, God can say, "OK, go this way. Now turn this way."

My dad always said that you cannot steer a bicycle that is not moving. It is time we got that bicycle going. It is time we stepped out and took some risks. The wealthy are risk takers.

Does that mean you will never fail? Absolutely not. The wealthy have failed hundreds of times more than you and I. That is why they are wealthy.

 The wealthy know that failing does not make you a failure. Never trying does.

Robert Kiyosaki, best-selling author of *Rich Dad Poor Dad*, said that nine out of ten businesses fail. We hear that and say that means the odds are stacked against us. We should stay away from that. We say, "I have a 90 percent chance that I will fail."

The wealthy say, "I have a 100 percent chance that I will succeed. I only have to start ten businesses to be a success."

It didn't matter that you failed on your first nine business ventures because on the tenth, you made $10 million.

Very few people have failed as many times as Donald Trump, yet he is far from being a financial failure.

 We see risks as something we can't afford to take. The wealthy see risks as something they can't afford not to take.

For the last ten years of my life, I was just like the rest of the Body of Christ. I was waiting for something to fall down on me, hoping the job would give me a raise. But it didn't matter how much money I made, at the end of the month, like everybody in America, I had the same amount left over. As I began to step out and think differently, my life began to change.

At one point, I thought I was taking a huge risk by getting into a million-dollar project. One year later, I had over $13 million worth of projects. What happened is that I started to think like a billionaire. I used to say that I can't afford to do that. Now I say I can't afford not to.

One of my partners spoke to me a few months into this process. He is a very intelligent man, a financial mentor of mine. He said, "We need to buy more."

"Whoa," I responded, "hold on 'Daddy' Warbucks. We already have $3 million going. That is enough."

He said, "There is a window of opportunity, and life is all about windows. Windows of opportunity open up for a brief period, and then they are gone. If we don't step into those windows of opportunity, we will miss them."

If I hadn't stepped in last year where I stepped in, I would have missed the opportunity to make an amazing amount of money in real estate. I would have just held on to one investment. I would have made some money, but by stepping out I have made a tremendous amount.

Wisdom: Books, CDs

It is amazing to me that the wealthy think differently about books and videos and CDs. The average American reads one book a year—I am not talking love stories or *People Magazine*, I am talking about a self-help motivating book.

The wealthy read an average of two a week. I read somewhere that Donald Trump reads two books a week—and he's got billions of dollars.

The wealthy know that wisdom is a key to abundance. They have a burning desire for more information on every area of investing from real estate to stocks to business. They constantly want to know how they can get more information on investing. The rich don't waste their time listening to mindless radio in their cars. Instead they say, "That's an hour a day, five hours a week, 25 hours a month, 300 hours a year, 15,000 hours in a lifetime (equivalent to 24 hours a day for two years straight) that I could spend listening to CDs and audio downloads that could benefit my life." Radio is not doing anything for their lives, but these audio messages deliver the wisdom that gets them not only to think, but also to produce differently.

What is amazing is that I have the exact same amount of time in my life for doing the things I was doing before. I just gave up the one hour of mindless listening to music. I don't even miss that hour. Now when

I get out of the car, I feel different. I feel changed. I feel like I have done something with my day, and it hasn't even started.

 We think that self-help books are a last resort to fixing the problem. The wealthy see them as the start to not having a problem.

Time

The wealthy have a whole different way of thinking about time. We just pass the time away. We waste time. We let others steal our time. To the wealthy, time is their most valuable asset.

We think money is the most valuable thing. The wealthy say, "I can get more money, but I can never get more time."

To the wealthy, time is an irreplaceable resource. It is the only limited resource they have. You can replace everything in life except for your time.

You can steal the wealthy person's money. "No big deal. I can get more money."

You can take his possessions. "I can get more possessions."

The wealthy will not allow you to ever steal their time because time is something they can never replace.

We go through life allowing people to steal our time. We do things in our own lives that waste our time. I'm not talking about taking vacations or having hobbies, things that you do to relax. There's nothing wrong with unwinding by watching a football game. Those things are vital tools to recharge you and keep your mind fresh. As you will see, we do things that have no benefit to our lives whatsoever. Time is something we think we have a lot of, so we give it away, throw it away.

Once again, to the wealthy, time is the most valuable thing they have. They remove time wasters from their lives. They stop doing things that waste their time.

Here is an example where we all live. You may have said or thought, "Look at that guy with his gardener taking care of his lawn and his maid cleaning the house. If I had that kind of money, I wouldn't waste it on that. I would give that money to the poor." It is that thinking that keeps you from having that money.

The wealthy say, "With the time I save not doing my own lawn, I can make thousands of dollars. The time I save not cleaning my house, I can use to make millions over my lifetime. I am also giving into a business, giving that business the opportunity to invest and succeed."

We spend 20 hours of frustration and $500 at Home Depot to paint the inside of our house by ourselves. When we get done, it looks like an amateur did it. If we paid someone a thousand dollars to do it and took that time and invested it, we would be so much further ahead.

We have a "just-get-by" attitude rather than seeing time the way the wealthy see it. Those 20 hours are way too valuable to me. To be able to buy 20 hours of time for $500 is a great deal for me.

I used to battle it out with my pool every week, plus I spent $30 or more a month on chemicals. Now, for $70 a month, I have someone do it for me. For $40 a month, I bought five hours of time. I used to spend two hours a week doing my lawn. Now, for $150 a month, my lawn is done for me. I bought eight hours of time for $150. I then use that time researching, looking at, and giving into my investments. In the last year, my greatest returns came from the investments I put my time into.

Summing It Up

We have to change our entire mindset. If we can change how we think, we will change our lives. If we can think as billionaires, we begin to change everything in our lives, and all of a sudden, abundance just naturally flows out into our lives.

Take this journey with me. I guarantee that in one year, if you change your thinking, you will dramatically change your life.

Action Steps

√   Look at your monthly expenditures and find an area where you can cut back so you can use that money to invest.

√   "God will bless what you put your hands to." Think of an endeavor you can put your hands to—perhaps one you have been afraid to try in the past—and begin to step out in it.

√   Look at your daily schedule and find 30 minutes or more that you now spend listening to the radio or watching television. Start spending that time gaining wisdom about a business venture or improving your knowledge base.

√   Think of one thing that you could delegate to your children or hire someone to do so that you have time to be more productive.

Key points and personal adaption

Chapter 13

Inside Out

Change has a considerable psychological impact on the human mind. To the fearful it is threatening because it means that things may get worse. To the hopeful it is encouraging because things may get better. To the confident it is inspiring because the challenge exists to make things better. —King Whitney Jr.

To me, this book is very exciting, because I love change. Whether it is change in my life, or someone else's life, it excites me. Like some of you, I've read hundreds of books on gaining finances and gone to many seminars on becoming wealthy. Sure, a lot of books are just gimmicks. A lot of seminars are just big hoaxes to make those putting on the seminars wealthy. But I did read a lot of good books and went to a lot of seminars that had great tools for learning how to invest in land, real estate, stocks, and bonds. I, like some of you, spent $500, $1,500, or $8,000 each on such seminars. Yet after one month, six months, one year, two years, I was in the same financial place I was before. The only difference was I had $500, $1,500, or $8,000 less in the bank than I did before the seminars.

I got the principles. I got the tools on how to get wealth, but nothing inside of me changed. I found out how to make money investing, but still inside of me was a force stopping me from stepping out and taking risks. I still had the fear and the stress. I still had the anxiety—and all of this held me back from using the tools I was given.

The tools are important, but if you don't change the inside, you will never be able to elevate yourself on the outside of your life. What is going on outside of you is no more than a reflection of what is in you. You can change all you want outside of you. You can change jobs, change marriages, change addresses, but it will seem that nothing has changed in your life. That is because what is in you is creating your world. You need to change the inward man, and then the outward man begins to produce.

So you went to seminar after seminar, and you got some great tools. You left pumped up and excited. You went home and told your spouse what you were going to do. You told him/her about the money you would make.

But a few weeks later, it came time to step out. It came time to put some money down, start that company, or buy that land. And then what was in you began to come out. You said things like, "Well, the economy is really bad right now. You know, the market is no good. Right now isn't a good time to start a business. I don't know if this invention is that good. Books are hard to get published. You know what? Let's hold off and wait. Maybe next year will be a better time." And one year, two years down the road, you are still in the same financial situation. You're still just getting by in your life.

The sad thing is, during that one or two years of wasting time, over 100,000 people became millionaires, using those principles that you said wouldn't work, during an economy you said was horrible, with that same invention you said no one would want, starting the business that you said couldn't make it. More than 100,000 people last year became millionaires, and the only difference between them and those who did not is simple. Those who became millionaires thought differently than those who did not. It had nothing to do with their past or their I.Q. It was a simple difference of what was in them. The millionaires were able to step out and take a risk. Those who did not become millionaires had reasons not to take the risks. Those who became millionaires found ways to succeed; those who did not found reasons not to try.

It is time you realize that you will never go beyond what is in you. As you will see, your subconscious will sabotage your circumstances, ideas, and life to keep you at the level your mind is at now. It will hold you back. You want more, but your subconscious will not allow you to get more. That's why 90 percent of the people who win the lottery go broke in a short time. Within five years, they are at the same place that they were before they won the money. Why is that? If you watch their lives, they are making bad decisions, horrible investments, squandering their money, and sabotaging their lives. Their subconscious is working 24 hours a day to get them back to their comfort zone. They may not like being broke, but they feel more comfortable being broke. What is in you will always come out of you.

How many sports stars do we see who make a fortune while they are playing, only to end up selling insurance later in life? Why is it that 75 percent of NFL players go bankrupt within the first five years of retiring from football? They are making millions of dollars only to wind up broke. Frequently, it is because they went beyond what was in them, and their subconscious took them right back to their comfort level.

You can finish this book a millionaire—a millionaire on the inside. You can get rid of everything in you that has been limiting your life—those fears, those wrong thoughts, those limiting beliefs—gone. Now you can step out of your old life and step into the life you desire. You will change your life from the inside out.

"But changing me won't teach me what to do."

I would say everybody reading this book, deep down inside, knows how to get rich. You know that the only difference between you and the rich person is the way you think. You read about the guy who made $20 million on an Internet idea and, you think, "I had that idea." "I had that invention five years ago." "I had an idea for that same business." Or you look at all the real estate deals out there and think, "I thought about putting aside money to invest in property. Why didn't I do it?"

You knew what to do. That isn't the problem. The problem is stepping out and doing it. The difference between you and the guy who made millions on the invention is one thing: he stepped out and did it. Why didn't you? Because what was in you held you back, while what was in him forced him forward.

Financially, Donald Trump is a very smart, gifted man, but inside of you are characteristics and gifts that he doesn't have. Many of you are smarter than he is in certain areas. You are gifted in areas he is not. You have talents he does not possess. Why is he a billionaire, and you are not? Because he thinks differently. Because of the way he thinks, he produces a different world.

You could take all of Trump's money away, and in a matter of time he would be a billionaire again. Why? Because of the way he thinks.

*You have to think anyway, so why not think **big!***
—Donald Trump

We think small. We think just enough to get by. Trump thinks big—too much, more than enough. We think of just getting a better job. Trump thinks of getting another multi-billion dollar deal. We look at a business and say, "Too big of a risk to do it." Trump looks at the same business and says, "Too big of a risk not to do it."

"Well, it's because of his connections, who he is, and who he knows."

You could take away his identity, you could change his face, take him out of where he is, and I guarantee you, in a matter of time, he would be a billionaire again. You could make him Scot Anderson. It would take a lot of work to make him look this good. We would make him 5'4" (have to cut him off at the knees). Now, you put him in my situation, with my resources, everything I have, and in a short amount of time, he would be a billionaire. Inside of me, I am still changing. Sure, I think like a millionaire, but now I have to take it to the next level and think like a billionaire.

He could become you, with your same gifts and talents. Trump could step into your identity, same money, problems, and circumstances. In a matter of time, he would be a billionaire. Why? Because he thinks differently.

I don't care if you are a single mom. Make Trump a single mom of four, living on welfare. In a matter of time he would be a billionaire. It might take a little longer, since he would have four kids to care for, but it would still happen. Because of the way he thinks!

This should excite you. This says if you can change how you think, you can change what you have. Get yourself thinking like a millionaire, and you will produce millions of dollars.

Action Steps

√ Write out the thoughts and fears that have prevented you from stepping out. Be honest with yourself. Now consider the advantages of stepping out and the regrets you will have if you never try. Which are more important?

√ List ideas you've had that could have been successful if only you had done them. Next, list some things you can do now that could become a big success in the future.

√ Begin to step out this week on one of those ideas.

Key points and personal adaption

_____

_____

_____

_____

_____

_____

_____

_____

_____

_____

_____

_____

_____

Chapter 14

The Power of Belief

You have powers you never dreamed of. You can do things you never thought you could do. There are no limitations in what you can do except the limitations in your own mind as to what you cannot do. Don't think you cannot. Think you can. —Darwin P. Kingsley

You possess one of the most powerful instruments in the universe! Every single person reading this book needs to realize that he/she has this instrument available right now. This instrument has over 20 billion cells, connected to over 20,000 other cells. This instrument has the capability of generating over 1,000,000,000,000,000,000,000,000,000,000,000, 000,000,000,000,000,000... (continue those zeros for over eight pages) thoughts, ideas, and insights. Experts say that the number of ideas you can have are more than all the molecules in the universe. And this is for the least intelligent person reading this book.

I am, of course, talking about your brain. The human mind is the most untapped resource in the universe. The capabilities that your mind possesses are so great, you have only scratched the surface of its potential—using less than 1 percent of it.

Even if you are the least intelligent person, you possess an unbelievable amount of power that is able to—and will—produce millions of dollars during your life—*if you allow it to!* If you take the limits off of it. The only thing that can limit your life is you! If you can remove those limits, you step into a world where, "If you can dream it, you can do it!"

The only way to discover the limits of the possible is to go beyond them into the impossible. —Arthur C. Clarke

What has to be exciting is that you have been born into a time of limitless resources and opportunities—as long as you don't listen to the media. The media said last year that the economy was horrible, yet 100,000 people became millionaires. Right now, in this time, we live in the wealthiest era the world has ever known. They say there are over 2 million millionaires, and the number continues to grow. Will you be one of them? The only person who can decide that is you!

The lack of opportunity is ever the excuse of a weak, vacillating mind. Opportunities! Every life is full of them. Every newspaper article is an opportunity. Every client is an opportunity. Every sermon is an opportunity. Every business transaction is an opportunity. —Orison Swett Marden

Today you have the opportunity to start down the path of wealth. You have the opportunity to become better at all you do. You have the opportunity to become a better spouse, a better parent, a better friend, a better son or daughter. You have the opportunity to be one step closer to success in all areas of your life.

Your life is full of opportunities. Today, tomorrow, the next day, and the day after that, each day contains 24 hours of opportunities. Will you continue to let them pass you by out of your limiting thinking? Or will you tap into the limitless gifts you have been given and seize the opportunities that will take you to your dreams and desires?

It is time you realize that you were engineered for success. You were created to be successful. You are one of a kind. There has never been anyone like you, and no one will ever be like you again. You have gifts and talents that are second to nobody else in this world. You have unbelievable abilities inside of you. If you can take those limits off of yourself, accept that you can, believe that you can, your life will begin to produce.

> *There is nothing on earth you cannot have—once you have mentally accepted the fact that you can have it.* —Robert Collier

That's good. There is nothing you can't do. There is nothing that you can't overcome. There is nothing that you can't have. It all becomes possible when your mind accepts that you can do it or have it.

Think about this: there are thousands of people out there who are not as smart as you who are millionaires. There are probably a half a million people out there who are not as gifted as you are, yet they are millionaires. There are so many people out there who had a worse childhood, had bigger circumstances to overcome than you. They had a worse past than you, yet they have millions in the bank. The only difference between them and you is the way you think. If you begin to think like they do, your life will begin to produce it naturally.

Nearly every study done to date concerning financial success has the same answer. Financial success has nothing to do with a person's I.Q. or with a person's gifts and talents. It has nothing to do with their past, or with their circumstances. People who are financially successful think differently.

It Is Like a Magnet

You take a piece of iron and magnetize it and that piece of iron can lift 12 times its weight. You demagnetize that iron, and it can't even lift a feather. It won't lift anything. It's interesting that in the world today there are two types of people. There are those whose minds have become magnetized. Their minds are full of confidence, magnetized with faith and expectation, and they are able to step out and do it. Their minds attract the ideas, the resources, and the people they need to be successful. Their minds work just like a magnet. They accomplish more than 12 times what the average person can do.

Then you have the other 95 percent of the people in the world today. Their minds have been demagnetized by what their parents said or by what their teachers said about them, demagnetized by what the media said, by their own limiting beliefs. They are full of fear, worry, and doubts. Their minds, in a way, push away success. They keep resources, ideas, and people at a safe distance. They just get by. They continue to live just average lives, far below the possibilities of what they should be able to have.

In just a short period of time, your mind can be magnetized. Then your mind will begin to draw everything you need to it. It will attract the people, the resources, the ideas, and the finances you need to accomplish your financial goal.

Deep down inside of you, what you believe is what your mind draws to it. If you believe you can't, guess what? Your mind will draw to it everything you need so you don't.

Whatever you believe with conviction, your mind will move Heaven and earth to make true. Your mind will work 24 hours a day to produce it.

Let me give you an example of how your mind brings what's in you into your reality. The Super Bowl is coming up, and you have been thinking about a big screen television for the last nine months. A few months ago, you accepted the fact that you can have a big screen television. Your spouse, on the other hand, has not accepted this fact. You know that right now the finances aren't where you want them to be, so you tell yourself, "Not now." But your mind begins to work 24 hours a day, trying to bring this into your world. It seems like everywhere you turn, you see ads for televisions and articles about televisions. The magnet has been activated. Two weeks before the Super Bowl, you are driving around doing errands when you look up and there is a Best Buy. You think to yourself, "Let's just go in and look around a little." Two hours later you are driving home with your 65" top-of-the-line big screen television that you financed for the next 72 years. Your only problem in life is explaining to your spouse what happened.

I will tell you what happened. Your subconscious mind was activated by your faith, beliefs, and your expectations. Your mind then began to draw everything you needed to bring into existence what was placed in it: "Now faith is the substance of things hoped for, the evidence of things not seen" (Heb. 11:1). Using that same principle, we will tap into that same power, and use it to bring the wealth you desire into your life.

Your mind takes you to what you believe. Understand it does not take you to where you want to go, but to where you believe. Your mind will always prove what you believe is true.

That's why a lot of people want lots of money, but deep down they believe they can't produce it. They think that because they aren't smart enough, don't have enough talent, or because of their past, it's something they can't have.

If you believe that you can't, your mind continues to prove that you can't. You're a failure because Mom and Dad said, "You are a failure, no good, and worthless." So you continue to produce failure into your life. You think you are just average because Daddy said, "Just work a job, and don't try to step out. Don't try to, because the economy is never any good. And you know, wealthy people,

they are unhappy. Money causes problems in your life."
Maybe some religion told you money was evil. So you
have that belief on the inside of you, and your mind says,
"I don't want to be evil, so let's not get a lot of money." Or
you believe, "I'm not smart enough," so your mind proves
to you throughout the day how unintelligent you are.

Your mind will block out anything that contradicts
what you believe.

For example, deep down you believe you are a failure. So your mind will not allow you to see the 35 successes that you had that day. It can only focus on the two
failures.

You believe that you're not smart enough, so anything smart you do, your mind does not show you. It is
just the dumb things that you do (we all do these) that
your mind lets you see. But the only difference between
you and a multimillionaire is that the multimillionaire
focuses on the smart things he/she does and you focus on
the unintelligent things you do.

Your mind blocks out all that is against what your
belief system is. What you believe on the inside of you is
what is producing in your life throughout the day. If you
change your belief system, you begin to change what
happens.

What is interesting about this is that it does not matter if what you believe is true or not. If it is true to you,

it is true. You may think you are not smart enough. That is totally untrue. But if it is true to you, it becomes your reality. Money is not evil, but if it is evil to you, then all you see in the media and in your neighbor's life is how money destroys.

But compare that with someone like me who sees money as an amazing tool to bless others. I see all the good money does—such as Bill Gates spending billions of dollars to make the world a better place—I see the money as good.

What you believe will always become your reality!

Let me give you an example:

Take a woman who believes that men are jerks because her dad left when she was young. She was abused by other male relatives. Throughout her whole life, men have always abused her and have always left her. We all probably know a woman like this. It seems like any guy she ever dates or marries is a jerk.

Is she just unlucky? No, it is her belief system. She believes all men are jerks, so her mind will only allow the jerks into her life. You can bring two men into her life. Both men are very handsome, 5'4" tall, sandy brown hair styled out of the eighties. You know the guy (his picture is next to his bio on the cover if you need a mental picture). One man would make an amazing husband. He would love and care for her. He would be true to her, be her prince charming. The other guy is a bum. Life is all about him. He has never been true to any woman. The only time he will come around is when there is nothing else to do. He'll never call her and basically treat her like dirt.

I ask you, which one will she pick every time? We both know she will pick the jerk. It doesn't matter that the good guy is buying her flowers, chasing her, trying to be the man she needs. Her mindset is, "Why is he all up in my business, smothering me, calling me all the time, getting me flowers and gifts?" (Because, of course, who would want that abuse?) "I just want to be friends with him. He isn't my type." The problem is she has the wrong type in her. She needs to change her type.

You see, she is attracted to the bum who never calls, who is out at the clubs all the time, and who wants nothing to do with her. This is the man she wants. She finally gets him, and a few years of abuse later, he leaves, thus proving to her that all men are jerks. Is that statement true? Absolutely not. But it is true to her because it is what she believes.

Here's another example:

You believe that you are unlucky in your investments. You believe that what you try in the financial world fails. It is your belief. So two deals present themselves to you. One is a money-maker, and the other is a dog. Which one will you pick every time? You will pick the dog, thus proving to you that you lack the chromosome needed to make money.

I have a good friend who believes this very thing. For the past decade he has told me how everything he invests in goes to garbage. I watch his life, and it is absolutely true. If he buys a stock, it is a guarantee that the company is going bankrupt soon. I actually tell him to let me know what stocks he will be buying so I can sell. I know he was responsible for each of the stock market crashes in the last fifteen years! I told him he could make a lot of money by just calling companies and telling them that if they don't give him $10,000, he will purchase their stock. Honestly, anything he invests in fails.

A couple of years ago I had invested in nine properties. I had a great deal on another property drop in my lap. This friend of mine had seen how much money I was making and told me he wanted in. I was maxed out at the time, so I presented it to him. I had everything in place for him—all he needed was $5,000 down. He put the money down.

One hour before he was to sign the papers, he called and said, "I can't do it. Too much stress. I can't handle it. I want out."

I said to him, "You are going to lose your $5,000, plus what you would make."

He said, "I don't care. I want out."

He got out, lost his money, but also lost over $100,000 he would have made on the deal. What happened? His subconscious would not allow him to get into a deal that went against his belief system. So it sabotaged him. Since then, he has invested in a lot of other bad investments. He just stays away from the good ones.

Some of you out there have had business opportunities, stocks you should have bought, inventions you should have done, things you should have been doing, things you knew would make you money. But your subconscious would not allow you to go against what you believe on the inside. If you can switch that around to where you believe that whatever you do is successful, that you are a money-maker, that wealth is attracted to you, all of a sudden, what you believe becomes your reality.

I believe I have blessing and favor in whatever I do. I believe that whatever I touch seems to turn to gold. In my life, that is exactly what happens. My mind takes me to all the good deals, all the great things. My mind works 24 hours a day to bring success into existence.

Starting today, your mind can be dragging you to success!

Action Steps

√   Make a list of all the successes you have had in the last year, in any area of your life. Don't stop until you have at least 20 things written down.

√   Think about choices you have made in your life. Are there any patterns of failure? What lies have you been believing? Repent to God for believing them.

√   Meditate on Hebrews 11:1. What dreams do you want to become a reality? Imagine what it would be like if they were real.

√   Take one step toward success today.

Key points and personal adaption

Chapter 15

Habits Control Your World

*The beginning of a habit is like an invisible
thread, but every time we repeat the act we
strengthen the strand, add to it another filament,
until it becomes a great cable that binds us irrevocably
in thought and act.* —Orison Swett Marden

Let's start out with the basics. I believe this will bring
a level of understanding that many of you have not
had before.

There are two parts to the mind: the conscious and
the subconscious. The conscious is the part of the mind
that chooses what you will believe. The subconscious
then directs the life based upon the beliefs that have been
written upon it (see Prov. 4:23).

Before you can succeed, you have to understand how
much of your life is controlled by your subconscious.

Most psychologists say that 95 percent of the decisions you make in a day are subconscious—an automatic response. That means that nearly all of the choices, decisions, feelings, and actions that you experience during the day are reactions that you don't think about.

Your spouse says something; you just respond. You have these natural responses inside of you that just continue to come out your whole life. They've been set in there since you were 12 years old; these cruise control responses guide how you operate 95 percent of the time.

That is why a lot of investing books don't work. They have great information, but you only use that information 5 percent of the time. You read the book, come up with all the things you are going to do, and then 5 percent of your day you do it, while the other 95 percent of your time is spent sabotaging it. You never seem to get anywhere. You say, "I am going to make these new choices and decisions." But that is only 5 percent of the time. Five percent of the time you are going in the right direction, and then the other 95 percent of the time your little vehicle turns around and goes the other way. You are never getting any closer to the direction that you want.

What are natural responses? Somebody cuts you off, pulls in front of your car. You have a natural response, right? It just comes right out of you! You didn't have to think about it—because if you did, you wouldn't have responded that way. You didn't say to yourself, "OK, now, raise your right hand. Extend your middle finger. Now, with your mouth, say, "#$@!" No, it just happens. It's almost like you had no control.

A business opportunity comes up. Right off the bat you say, "Oh, not right now."

You get an invention idea. "No, I can't do that."

A management position opens up. "Not for me. I'm not smart. I'm not intelligent enough." You don't even have to think about it; it just comes right out of your subconscious.

Repeat anything long enough and it will start to become you. —Tom Hopkins

If you change that subconscious reaction from negative to positive—from taking you away from what you want instead of toward what you are supposed to be having—you will begin to go subconsciously toward the life you dream of.

Your subconscious mind is like the hard drive of a computer. It's been preprogrammed with things. If you hit the letter "Q" on a computer, a "Q" is going to pop up. You get in there, and you double click on AOL, AOL is going to come up. You double click on Word, Word will pop up. Every action has a set reaction in your computer.

Your life is the same thing. When a button is pushed in your life, you have a natural reaction to it.

What is interesting about the computer is you can get into the hard drive and mess with the reaction. Some buddies and I wanted to tease a good friend of ours. So we went on his computer and changed it so every time he typed the word *the*, the word *sex* was put into its place. He would finish a letter, and *sex* would be in it 20 times. "Bro, you need to get your mind out of the gutter!" we would tell him.

Inside all of us, we have areas where our *the* doesn't produce what we want. You type in *the*, trying to get to success, and it takes you to failure. Your job in this book is to get your actions and reactions to take you to success.

The conscious mind chooses what you believe— what you believe you can do, what you can have, the talents and gifts you possess, your opinions, and your views on money, relationships, life in general. The sad thing is that most of these choices were made by the time you were 12 years old. Most of these opinions and beliefs came from what your parents told you, what your teachers, friends, the media, and even your enemies said about you or to you. A lot of those things were lies. These beliefs were then written upon your subconscious mind. The subconscious mind then uses this information to direct your life.

Unfortunately, your subconscious mind never argues with the conscious mind. It takes as fact whatever you tell it. If you tell it that you're worthless, it says, "OK, I am worthless." It then makes decisions based out of that belief. Please remember that its goal is to prove true what you believe. Your subconscious shows you all the worthless things you do and sabotages circumstances in your life to prove to you that you are worthless. Are you worthless? Of course not! But what you choose to believe has the power to change your life. What God once said to Israel, He also says to you, "I have loved you with an everlasting love; ... with lovingkindness I have drawn you" (Jer. 31:3). It is impossible that God should love what has no worth; His love *bestows* worth. Choose to believe that!

Your subconscious becomes the cruise control of your life. It makes most of your choices and most of your decisions. Your subconscious is putting forth your attitude, dictating how you respond and react to circumstances in your life. It is creating your world from the inside out.

Habit is either the best of servants or the worst of masters. —Nathaniel Emmons

Let me give you an example of the power of the subconscious mind. Remember, much of what you believe was put inside of you by parents, teachers, and peers by the time you were 12. Those beliefs still dictate your life today.

When I was between six months and nine months old, according to my parents, I loved fudgesicles, candy bars, and Fudge Pops. Every time Mom would open up the goodies, I would get all excited! For three months they gave me lots of chocolate.

At nine months old, they gave me a fudgesicle, I ate the whole thing, and for whatever reason, I got really sick and threw it up. The next day, when they took out a fudgesicle, I wouldn't even put it in my mouth. This made my parents come to the conclusion that I did not like chocolate. (Why? I have no clue, since I had loved chocolate for the prior three months.) So, from that moment on, my parents began to say, "Scot does not like chocolate." That is what they began to speak over my life. As long as I can remember, I was told I hated chocolate. At 12 years old, I had a friend ask, "Have you ever tried chocolate?" I thought for a second and said, "Not since I was nine months old."

Isn't it interesting how your parents can put a belief inside of you, and you never try it, you never test it? You just assume it is true and live your life around the belief. You were told, "You're not smart." You never tested that. You were told to just get a job and work your life away. You never tested that. You were told that wealthy people are snobs and look down on people. You never tested that. Your parents said, "You can't succeed." You just took that for fact. Your parents said, "You will never amount to anything," and you just believed it.

The subconscious mind will always prove itself true. So when I tried a piece of chocolate, of course, I hated it. Because it is what I believed. "Well, Scot, maybe you really didn't like chocolate." Maybe, but this next part dismisses that theory.

Growing up, I loved ice cream sandwiches. They were my favorite thing. I remember when I was in sixth grade going to Grandpa's house for three weeks. He bought a huge box of 50 ice cream sandwiches. I ate all of those in a week.

I remember Grandpa saying to me, "Boy, you love those things don't you?"

I said, "Yep."

He said, "But don't you hate chocolate?"

I said, "Yes, but what does that have to do with ice cream sandwiches?"

He said, "Those wafers are chocolate."

I said, "Grandpa, no, they are not. If they were, I would hate ice cream sandwiches."

He said, "Oh."

And we went on with our lives. I continued to eat all the ice cream sandwiches I could get my hands on.

Then I got married. One day while eating my second ice cream sandwich, my wife asked, "How can you eat that? It's chocolate."

Once again, I said, "No, it is not."

My wife, who, unlike my grandfather, could not just be wrong and let me enjoy my true passion, grabbed the box out of the freezer and showed me where it said "chocolate wafers."

All of a sudden the sandwich tasted funny. I told her I liked the ones without the chocolate wafers. (I have yet to find those, and I have been looking for the last ten years.) And since then I have not been able to eat an ice cream sandwich. That is the power of the subconscious mind. As soon as my mind figured out that was chocolate, it told me, "Well, I don't like them; I can't eat that."

Your parents said many things that got down into your subconscious, a lot of which probably is not true. You can't back it up with any fact, but you believe it as true. Even though it is not true, it becomes true to you. And so you continue to make choices based on lies. You continue missing the chocolate of life—the good things of life—because of something Mom said when you were seven years old, or something that your teacher said in the first grade.

A belief is not just an idea that you possess; it is an idea that possesses you. —John Maxwell

Go back to the computer example. We have preprogrammed responses inside of us. These are called habits. These habits dictate what we experience and the life we produce.

Inside of your subconscious are these habits that drive your life. It's the cruise control that takes you places. You have the habit of how you respond to every situation in your life. If you could change the habits, your life would naturally go where you wanted it to go. If you could get the habits of Trump, you would become like Trump. If you could act like a successful person, even 95 percent of the time, you would become successful.

The programming that you accept from others, and the conscious and unconscious directives, pictures, feelings, and thoughts that you transmit to yourself, will find a place in your own internal control center. Together, those thoughts and images will continue to create action that will be a part of you and your future. —Dr. Shad Helmstetter

This book is all about changing the habits inside of you. Once you do, you can get millionaire habits. It is interesting that you can ask any self-made multimillionaire, "OK, how did you get that first million?"

And he will say, "You know what? It was a lot of work. I had to work and change a lot of things inside of me. There were a lot of habits and a lot of wrong beliefs that I changed in here that got me that first million. But that second million came really easy. And that third million was even easier."

Why? Because once you change the habits to get the first million, those same habits continue to produce the next million and the next million in your life.

As soon as you change the habits inside, you will see your life begin to change right away.

I have heard it said many times:

We first make our habits and then our habits begin to make us. —John Dryden

If you can get the habits of a successful person, you will become successful. If you can get the habits of a happy person, you will become happy. If you can get the habits of a millionaire, you will become a millionaire.

Most physiologists will agree that it takes 21 days to form a habit. If you will just invest 21 days, you can change your life. In 21 days you can think like a millionaire. Then you will have the habits of a millionaire, and from those habits you will produce millions of dollars.

You really can become the person who makes your dreams into realities!

Action Steps

√ List one or more negative things you were told as a child or that you believe today. Now write out three Scriptures that prove why this negative belief is untrue about you.

√ Think of at least one thing you're not good at or don't like. Test that thought to see if it's really true.

√ Mark out 21 days on your calendar. Every day meditate on the success Scriptures that you wrote out above. Reject any thoughts from your subconscious that disagree with the Word. Keep this up until you are thinking success subconsciously.

Key points and personal adaption

_____

_____

_____

_____

_____

_____

_____

_____

_____

_____

_____

_____

_____

_____

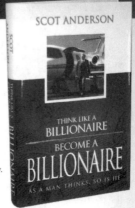

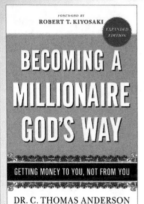
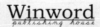